'This warm and wonderful book will be a tremendous help to very many Christians seeking to understand and to pray the psalms in Christ. In my experience, books about the psalms tend either towards dry scholarship lacking in the richness of Christ or to popular devotion lacking in depth. This book is built on careful scholarship and grapples with the text in the context of the whole Bible with Christ at its centre. But it combines these scholarly foundations with a warm pastoral tone and an understanding of how the psalms engage with the life of faith in Christ today. I am so thankful for it and warmly commend it.'
Christopher Ash, Writer-in-Residence, Tyndale House, Cambridge.

'The psalms are always spiritually refreshing, but it is easy to read them superficially. This book shows us how to read the psalms deeply in their Old Testament and biblical context as poetry full of imagery and emotions. It brings scholarly understanding (of course) but more than that, it takes us through a spiritual story and shows us how walking in Christ's way is deeply satisfying and worth any sacrifice. Reading this, we are brought to the God who walks every step of the way with us. If you want to be "the tree whose leaf does not wither", this book shows you how.'
Kirsten Birkett, author of *Living Without Fear: Using the Psalms to End your Fear and Anxiety*

'With an ease that belies the expertise behind it, Shead fits each of his selected psalms into the grand history of Israel and into the grander history of those who follow Jesus. Satisfying to both scholar and common reader, here is a series of exquisitely crafted meditations that will delight the mind, nourish the heart, and quicken feet to *Walk His Way*.'
Havilah Dharamaj, Head of the Department of Biblical Studies, South Asia Institute of Advance Christian Studies

'Having had the privilege of hearing the talks on which this excellent book is based, I am delighted to be able to study them further in written form. This book will be a blessing to all who read it carefully and will draw you closer to the Lord.'

Dr Peter Jensen, former Archbishop of the Diocese of Sydney and Principal of Moore Theological College; husband, father and grandfather

'In *Walk His Way*, Andrew Shead shows himself to be the best of travel guides. Wise and superbly informed, but also compassionate and companionate. Recognizing that the psalms rate as many people's favourite part of Scripture, Shead unveils for us with clarity and sympathy the riches of God's 'hymnbook' for his people. One finds oneself continually refreshed and delighted by sparkling insights, not least of all concerning God's King, the Christ, the promise of whom is fulfilled in Jesus. The psalms selected for in-depth exposition (the chapters were originally given as talks) traverse the breadth of human experience, and the tension of living (or walking) by faith in a world wrecked by sin. The volume is worth having for the chapter on Psalm 88 alone. Here is a book on the psalms that will cause you to treasure, and meditate upon them, all the more.'

Kanishka Raffel, Archbishop of Sydney, Australia

'As I read the psalms, I often wish to have a spiritual tutor next to me, showing me the deeper meanings of what I am reading, how the Psalter is prayed by Jesus and with Jesus, and how some difficult texts may be reconciled with my own Christian experience. This small book by Andrew Shead serves the role of such a tutor. Through a selection of key psalms, the author offers a valuable lens through which to reflect on the Psalter theologically and prayerfully.'

Myrto Theocharous, Academic Dean and Professor of Hebrew and Old Testament, Greek Bible College, Pikermi, Greece

WALK HIS WAY

Andrew G. Shead gained his PhD from the University of Cambridge and is currently Head of Old Testament at Moore Theological College, Sydney. He has taught Hebrew poetry and the Psalms to many generations of students. He loves nothing better than to see eyes opened and lives touched through deep engagement with God's Word, whether it is in the classroom, in pastoral conversations or in the churches where he has served as an Anglican minister. Andrew is married with three young adult children, who fill his life with excellent conversation.

WALK HIS WAY

Following Christ through the book of Psalms

Andrew G. Shead

INTER-VARSITY PRESS
36 Causton Street, London SW1P 4ST, England
Email: ivp@ivpbooks.com
Website: www.ivpbooks.com

First published 2023

British Library Cataloguing-in-Publication Data
A catalogue record for this book is available from the British Library.

ISBN: 978–1–78974–478–1
eBook ISBN: 978–1–78974–479–8

Set in Minion Pro 11/14pt
Typeset in Great Britain by CRB Associates, Potterhanworth, Lincolnshire
Printed in Great Britain by Ashford Colour Press Ltd, Gosport, Hampshire

Produced on paper from sustainable sources

*Inter-Varsity Press publishes Christian books that are true to the Bible and that
communicate the gospel, develop discipleship and strengthen the church for its
mission in the world.*

*IVP originated within the Inter-Varsity Fellowship, now the Universities and Colleges
Christian Fellowship, a student movement connecting Christian Unions in
universities and colleges throughout Great Britain, and a member movement
of the International Fellowship of Evangelical Students. Website: www.uccf.org.uk.
That historic association is maintained, and all senior IVP staff and committee
members subscribe to the UCCF Basis of Faith.*

For Katie, David and Sophie

Contents

Illustrations

Introduction

The book of Psalms is a river of song. Each song is complete in itself, but the 150 songs that make up the book of Psalms have been carefully arranged to take us on a journey. The eight psalms we will be studying in this book are stopping-places from which we can map out the river's path – a path that travels through lament before it ends in praise. I hope that by the end of the journey we will feel that all the experiences of our lives, difficult as they may sometimes have been, have been steps along God's path to joy.

This book began life as a series of Bible talks given at the New South Wales CMS (Church Missionary Society) Summer School of 2022. Our aim was to engage deeply with God's Word so that we might know him better and follow Christ more faithfully. The Psalms are among the best-known and loved parts of Scripture. So how can we deepen our engagement with them? I have chosen three areas to focus on:

1 There is the overall story of the book of Psalms, within which each psalm finds its place. This is a story that has received much scholarly attention over the last thirty or forty years, and – unlike much biblical scholarship! – deserves to be widely known.
2 There is the art of reading poetry well. For many of us, poetry has remained a closed book since we 'did poetry' at school. But in God's wisdom a large percentage of the Bible is poetry, an art-form that requires us to slow down and read with disciplined imagination.
3 There is the rest of the Old Testament, whose law, history and prophecy provide the book of Psalms with its source-material. Recognizing how a psalm meditates on Scripture helps us

understand how it functions as prophecy of the Christ to come. The prophets and the apostles are our guides in this task, as they in turn meditate on the Psalms.

These three areas are typically addressed in the introductory sections of a theological course on the Psalms. But rather than turn these Bible studies into a 'Psalms 101' unit, I have chosen to devote some time in each study to an aspect of the larger story of the Psalms (area 1); and to model and illustrate the art of reading poetry and the use of the Old Testament in the Psalms (areas 2 and 3) as we go. By this method I hope that we will come away with a better sense of how the book of Psalms holds together, and how to read it and benefit from it as Christian Scripture.

Finally, I have decided to preserve the original form of these chapters as 'talks', and speak directly to you, the reader of this book. The book of Psalms does not address itself to just anyone. It is intended for people who would follow Christ along his path of trust and obedience. If we can place ourselves among the audience of the book of Psalms we will receive its message more clearly.

The title of this book was the theme of our summer school: 'Walk His Way'. Many of us, not only those working in cross-cultural mission, have given up so much to serve Christ. We make fools of ourselves in the world by following a path whose end we cannot see, because we have trusted a promise. When times get tough, we can find ourselves wondering if it's all been for nothing, if it's even real. We may doubt God, or ourselves, or those we work with.

My prayer is that the book of Psalms will help us reflect deeply on this path of faith and obedience, and take away a fresh vision of the God who walks it with us.

1

Psalms 1 and 2: the journey begins

Through the gates of the library

The book of Psalms is like a library spread across five interconnected rooms. I have sketched out these rooms in the empty diagram on page 3 (see Figure 2). Feel free to annotate it, if you would find that helpful. The five rooms are the five smaller 'Books' that make up the book of Psalms. These subdivisions are the work of the anonymous author of the book of Psalms. Most individual psalms have named authors, but Old Testament books do not. The book of Psalms contains psalms from the time of Moses to the time of Ezra, and many of them were in smaller collections before they got collected into the final edition. Think of it as Israel's hymnbook, getting new hymns added to it as the centuries wore on.

Once the author of the book of Psalms got all the psalms arranged into this five-room library, he placed two gateway psalms at the entrance, and five destination psalms at the exit. The destination psalms all begin and end with 'Hallelujah!', and we'll look at one of them in our final study. In this first study we will start with the two gateway psalms.

As the name 'gateway' suggests, Psalms 1 and 2 are the book's introduction. Unlike the psalms of David that follow them, they are untitled. Psalm 1 introduces us to the book's *purpose*, and Psalm 2 introduces us to the book's *theme* and *plot*.

So what is the purpose of the Psalms according to Psalm 1? Basically, to be a *path* through life that we should follow if we want to live well. Psalm 2 then describes the *journey* this path traces out, and it shows us that it's the king's journey first and foremost. Our job is to follow him. The theme of the book, according to Psalm 2, is the universal reign of the LORD and his anointed king in Zion. And so the plot is about how the LORD and his king come to reign supreme over all the nations (see Figure 1).

Psalm 1	Purpose	The Psalms trace a **path** through life
Psalm 2	Theme	The royal **journey** this path traces out
	Plot	How Zion's king comes to reign over the nations

Figure 1 **Purpose and plot of the Psalms**

As we come to Psalm 1, let me say a word about the art of reading psalms well. Psalms are poetry, and the first purpose of poetry in any language is to make the reader slow down. Every word in a poem has been carefully considered and precisely placed to present us with a world in miniature. There are shapes to the spaces created by the way ideas lie together. There are emotional journeys behind the flow of images. There are shifts of perspective that make us suddenly realize we need to go back and start again. So let's 'go slow' for a while as we enter the world of Psalm 1.

Psalm 1: the path

The path not taken (1:1)

Verse 1 is a portrait of the blessed person. Its three negative images are balanced by three positive images in verse 3, with a description of the blessed person's behaviour sandwiched in the middle. The whole portrait is bracketed by 'Blessed is the one' at the top, and 'whatever they do prospers' at the end of verse 3. Let's start with verse 1:

¹Blessed is the one
  who does not walk in step with the wicked
or stand in the way that sinners take
  or sit in the company of mockers¹

2

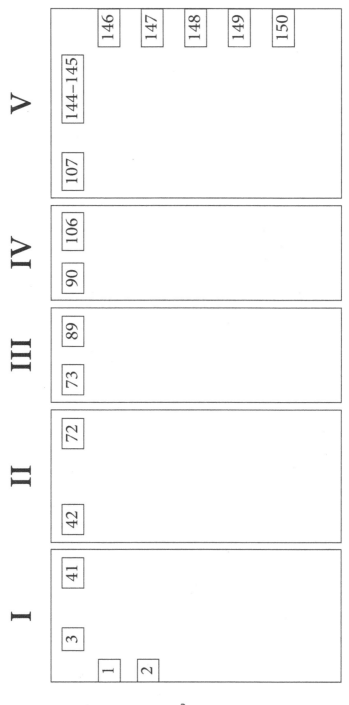

Figure 2 The five 'Books' of the Psalms

Walking, standing and sitting are three images of *identification*, of solidarity with the wicked. To 'walk in step' is to follow their advice. To 'stand in the pathway' is to share their way of life. To 'sit in their seat' is to share their judgments about the world, to adopt their attitude, their mindset. This is a mindset that boils down to 'mockery', a word that Proverbs uses to describe arrogant fools: people who are never wrong about anything, who never listen or take advice, who never admit to mistakes, who look down on everyone else.

The order of these images is unusual, because we'd have a better climax by reversing them: 'You need to get rid of the world's mindset! But don't stop there. Get rid of the world's lifestyle as well! In fact, just don't imitate *any* of the world's behaviour: do not walk in step with the wicked!' But these lines aren't building to a climax of disengagement. They're moving in the other direction to describe a journey of assimilation, a miniature story of a person who is slowly drawn in to the world of godless people.

After all, there is a lot of wisdom in the world's recipe for success. Get yourself on a solid footing, build some financial security, and you'll be in a better position to serve God, down the track. This might mean you have to look out for yourself for a while, make some alliances of convenience with certain types of people. These are cynical times, but pragmatism works. And soon you start to pull in some rewards, and you find yourself enjoying respect from the cool kids. You are on the inside now, telling jokes in the clubhouse and laughing at the little people. You know how the world works, and you can join with your mates to make sure the 'powers that be' tilt things your way. In fact, you most emphatically did it your way! And perhaps the people you naively wanted to help by staying poor and humble can have a building with your name on it when you die.

Psalm 73 almost despairs over the success of people like this, but here at the beginning of the book things are very clear. True happiness comes to the person whose life is not pointed in this direction. Instead, true happiness comes to the most unlikely person imaginable, to someone who on the face of it looks like a complete loser.

A strange obsession (1:2)

The opening word of verse 2 is an emphatic contrast:

> ²*but* whose delight is in the law of the Lord,
>   and who meditates on his law day and night.

'Law' is prominently named in both lines. It dominates the horizons of the blessed person. He or she is the ultimate law nerd, a law obsessive, a law binge-watcher. This is so strange to us, both as modern readers and also as Christians. The image of twenty-four-hour *meditating* – the word means muttering under your breath – seems more like the behaviour of an ultra-orthodox Jew than that of a Christian who is freed from bondage to the law. So it's important to think carefully about this verse.

The law of Moses

The word 'law' (*torah* in Hebrew) can mean a number of things, but here it clearly means the law of Moses: Genesis, Exodus, Leviticus, Numbers, Deuteronomy. In fact the language of Psalm 1 echoes God's instructions to Joshua after Moses died. God even uses the same poetic word for 'meditate' that we've seen in verse 2: 'Meditate on this book of the law day and night . . . and you will make your path prosper' (Joshua 1:8, my translation).

Make no mistake: the law of Moses was beautiful. It was a social charter unique in the ancient world, a blueprint for a just and equitable society where people could enjoy a fruitful existence in harmony with creation and with one another. But the books of the law don't just contain laws. They also contain the narrative of redemption that precedes the laws and gives them their rationale. A redemption story followed by instruction. That's the Mosaic law, and both the redemption story and the instructions revealed to Israel who God is: 'the compassionate and gracious God, slow to anger, abounding in love and faithfulness' (Exodus 34:6). The law placed the people of Israel into a relationship with that God. And it showed them what to do to say 'thank you' to God for rescuing them.

Christians aren't bound by the Mosaic law, because God didn't rescue us from slavery in Egypt. He rescued us from slavery to sin by the death of Christ. And in the New Testament we have our own redemption story followed by instruction. It's called the Gospels and the epistles. But here's the thing: the God each redemption story and each set of instructions reveals is one and the same God. To know the law – whether through Moses or the New Testament – is to know God, and to delight in the law is to delight in God. Psalm 1 calls Christians to delight in both Testaments, to delight in the God they reveal to us and to delight in obeying him as instructed by Christ.

Meditating on the law

But what about the second line of verse 2? What does a *meditation* on his law look like? Well, the answer to that is simple. It looks like a psalm. Let me show you a couple of clues to this.

The first and simplest clue is structure. The book of Psalms is divided into five smaller books as an echo of the five books of Moses. Its author wanted us to receive the Psalms as the Davidic *torah*, the law of David. To reinforce that, we find two psalms about the law in key positions: Psalm 19 at the centre of Book I, and Psalm 119 at the centre of Book V.

The second clue is the way psalms speak about the law. Here are some excerpts from Psalm 119:

Open my eyes that I may see
    wonderful things in your law.
(Psalm 119:18)

In the night, LORD, I remember your name,
    that I may keep your law.
(Psalm 119:55)

I long for your salvation, LORD,
    and your law gives me delight.
(Psalm 119:174)

The writer of Psalm 119 is acutely aware of his failings, and he sees the Mosaic law as the key to a restored relationship with God. There's nothing automatic about this. It's not about performing rituals to get himself forgiven. His heart is filled with love for God, and keeping the law is how he expresses that love.

The people of Israel as a whole did not love God. They preferred to serve themselves. But for some of them, including the psalm writers, the promise of the New Covenant that the law would be written on everyone's heart (Jeremiah 31:33) was already true. David describes these righteous Israelites in very bold terms:

The law of their God is in their hearts;
    their feet do not slip.
(Psalm 37:31)

This is why Christians, who may struggle to relate to a book such as Leviticus, feel so instinctively at home in the Psalms. The Israelites did not know God as well as we do, to whom the fullness of God is revealed in the person of the Lord Jesus. And yet an Israelite with a heart transformed by the law of Moses enjoyed the same relationship with God that we enjoy when our hearts are transformed by the gospel of Christ. And so the law of David speaks for members of both covenants equally.

The New Testament has a new redemption story, but it does not have a new book of songs. The Psalms already contain the words God has given us to express our dependence and trust and hope and love.

The law of David

Let's summarize what we've found. The blessed person meditates on the law of Moses. What does that look like? It looks like the book of Psalms. The law of David consists of 150 meditations on the law of Moses, the Scriptures. Those meditations are responses to God from hearts that have come to know him through the law.

Calling the Psalms 'the law of David' points to one final implication of verse 2. The meditations themselves are also law, not in the technical sense of Mosaic law but in the broader sense of authoritative teaching. The word *torah* sometimes has this broader sense, as when Asaph says, 'My people, hear my teaching (*torah*)' (Psalm 78:1). Psalm 1 is not a prayer. It gives advice for living. And its position at the head of the book points to the function of the Psalms as advice for living, authoritative teaching, the word of God.

By praying and singing and memorizing the Psalms, we learn to become the blessed person of verse 1: to walk in step with God, to follow his way of life, to take on his mindset.

I don't know how the Psalms feature in your devotional life, but this might be a good time to revisit that question and explore new ways of internalizing them, whether it's by reading, listening to audiobooks and podcasts, putting musical versions on a playlist, or – above all – incorporating them into your prayers. Here are some words from Dietrich Bonhoeffer to be going on with:

> When read only occasionally, these prayers are too overwhelming in design and power and tend to turn us back to more palatable fare. But whoever has begun to pray the Psalter seriously and regularly will soon give a vacation to other little devotional prayers.[2]

The traveller (1:3)

So far the poet has been describing the path to blessing. Now he switches to consider the traveller:

> [3]That person is like a tree planted by streams of water,
>   which yields its fruit in season
> and whose leaf does not wither –
>   whatever they do prospers.

Behind this description lies a very wise question. What sort of person will this journey make you? It's a great question for anyone to ask before they make big life choices, isn't it: what sort of person will this journey make you? Psalm 1 has a more specific version of the question: who do you become when you drink from the waters of the Psalms?

To answer this question the poet gives us the image of a tree. And, just like a tree, the image spreads luxuriantly across three lines of poetry. First we see the tree in all its splendour; then the camera focuses in on its abundant fruit, then right down to the detail of each green leaf. As our attention narrows, the setting expands, from a place (by streams of water), to a time (in due season), to timelessness (does not wither). We are reminded of the tree in Eden, which stood by the river that brought the life of God to the world.

What are the streams of water here in Psalm 1? They are the streams of *torah*, of the word of God, into which the blessed woman, the blessed man, sinks their roots. And as these life-giving words strengthen you, you bear fruit and become a source of life for others. And yes, there will be hard seasons: winter storms, long dry spells, searing heat. But they cannot sap the life from you, because your roots are sunk deep. It's a rich image, but its last line is a little difficult. A person like this, it claims, is not subject to futility. 'Whatever they do prospers.'

Really? Doesn't that feel as if we've crossed a line into triumphalism? Maybe it's poetic exaggeration. Well, I don't think so, not if you stay with the image. If a person draws their life up, out of the life of God the Creator, then life cannot help blossoming everywhere. It's an inevitable consequence. The puzzle is how to lay this image alongside real life, where pandemics and wars take the lives of healthy young people, and unscrupulous profiteers make their fortunes from the turmoil. Later psalms address this puzzle head-on, but even now I think we can make three points.

First of all, we should boldly embrace this claim. Christians who have given everything to serve Christ, who have known deprivation and suffering, almost always enjoy a richness of life, a sense of blessing and happiness, that they could never have known had they chosen to live from themselves.

Second, however, only one person ever lived completely from God. The Church Fathers who took the blessed one in this psalm as a prophecy of Jesus were not wrong. The rest of us may delight in the law of the LORD, but we drink from other waters too, and we all fall short of this ideal.

Third, even for Jesus the prospering of all his deeds did not mean wealth and happiness. It meant having no place to lay his head, and it meant dying the undeserved death of a criminal. There's no getting away from the tension in this psalm between appearance and reality. How do you even know which is which? The lifestyle of the wicked has all the appearance of happiness. The claims about the godly life have all the appearance of fraud. But the psalmist claims that the reality is the exact opposite. This tension between appearance and reality is a major theme in the Psalms.

Psalm 1 starts to address this tension by returning to the wicked, to examine what sort of person you become when you live from yourself rather than from God.

The destination: appearance versus reality (1:4–6)

The densely packed images of verse 3 give way to a single image in verse 4, spread thinly across two lines:

⁴They are like chaff
 that the wind blows away.

The wicked. They loomed so large and solid at the start, but they turn out to be hollow men. Dry, insubstantial, unnourishing, doing nothing, powerless to resist even a light breeze. These are people who have no source of life outside themselves, and so they have no substance. They have no place to stand outside themselves, and so they cannot act in the world. They can only be acted upon, blown this way and that.

Elsewhere in the Bible the image of chaff blown by the wind is an image of God's judgment, and judgment will bring the story of the wicked to an end in the last two verses of the psalm. Because they are people of no weight or substance, the wicked will be swept away before the wind of God's judgment, while the weighty grain remains in the winnowing pan.

The judgment of sinners happens on two levels in this psalm. First of all, society judges them. Verse 5 imagines their condemnation in court and their exclusion from the righteous community in Israel:

> ⁵Therefore the wicked will not stand in the judgment,
>   nor sinners in the assembly of the righteous.

And we shouldn't underestimate how often in real life crime doesn't pay. But in its context as an introduction to the whole book, I believe we are meant to extend this imagery towards God's judgment on the last day, with the assembly of the righteous being the saints gathered around God, as they are in some of the later psalms.

And of course it's on the last day that the veil of appearances will finally be stripped away, and the reality of each person's life made visible. On that day, all that the blessed person did will finally be seen to prosper, their faithfulness vindicated. For the time being, however, we live by faith. We trust the promise of verse 6:

> ⁶the LORD watches over the way of the righteous,
>   but the way of the wicked leads to destruction.

'The way of the righteous' describes, above all, the path Jesus walked, as the only truly blessed person born on this earth. But it's a path he walked so that we could follow behind him, with God's help.

We're called to walk a path whose destination we cannot see. But God knows every inch of that path. It's the path to his front door, and nobody who walks that path, that path of glad obedience, will fail to arrive safely at his house. No difficulty is unanticipated. No obstacle is too large for the path to cross, no temptation too wide to skirt, no discouragement too deep to traverse. We are never out of his sight, and in the darkness his word lights the way home. God watches your path.

The path of the righteous seems foolish to the world because it's a hard path and its end is hidden. By all appearances, the person who lives to know Christ and make him known has thrown away their chance of happiness and success for a fantasy. I was at college with a highly qualified engineer who gave the three decades of his greatest earning potential to live in an impoverished country, he and his family living for years without electricity or running water, doing work that nobody in the wider world will notice, sending their children to schools far away, subject to exotic diseases and second-class health care, almost dying once, without rights of citizenship, befriending locals who will never form completely normal relation-ships with them, cut off from extended family . . . What if it was all for nothing?

That's a question I imagine many of you may have asked your-selves during dark nights of the soul. It's a question that Psalm 1 has begun to answer, but for a full answer we need Psalm 2 as well. Our aim in the rest of this study is not to examine Psalm 2 thoroughly. We will simply explore how it fills out the message of Psalm 1.

Psalm 2: the journey

Psalm 2 is a drama in four scenes. It introduces us to the book's main characters: the LORD, his king, his enemies and, in the last line, those who take refuge in him – the people Psalm 1 calls 'the assembly of the righteous'. Each scene highlights one of these characters, and their interactions create a drama that points towards the climax of the whole book. Let's take a quick look.

Scene 1: earth (2:1–3)

Psalm 1 was a calm meditation on the Word of God. Psalm 2 is any-thing but calm. It's aggressive, shouty, uncomfortably hostile, as the LORD shirtfronts his enemies (as we say in Australia!):

> ¹Why do the nations conspire
>   and the peoples plot in vain?

The opening 'Why' is already scornful of the human project to break free from God's rule. It's a project that's the exact opposite of the project of meditation on God's law in Psalm 1. In fact the Hebrew word translated as 'meditate' in Psalm 1:2 is reused here in the opening verse of Psalm 2, where it means 'plot'. And that word-play turns Psalm 2 into a sequel, where the ultimate enemies of the blessed person are revealed. The wicked who gathered to mock God in Psalm 1 are dwarfed by this gathering. A groundswell of moral outrage has culminated in entire nations coming together, their rivalries set to one side in the face of a common enemy. These United Nations are gathered in a General Assembly because their human happiness and dignity, their fundamental freedoms, have been stripped from them by a foreign power.

But look who they're up against: the LORD and his anointed!

> ²The kings of the earth rise up
>   and the rulers band together
>   against the LORD and against his anointed, saying,
> ³'Let us break their chains
>   and throw off their shackles.'

What are the nations thinking? Just compare the opposing sides. In verse 1 the camera panned across the numberless host of God's enemies – an ocean of warriors from horizon to horizon. Now it zooms in until we are close enough to see individual kings and rulers and hear them speak. But when the camera points up to heaven, all we get to see is a distant figure, enthroned in glory.

Scene 2: heaven (2:4–6)

It's not God's face that silences the nations.

> ⁴ The One enthroned in heaven laughs;
>   the Lord scoffs at them.
> ⁵He rebukes them in his anger
>   and terrifies them in his wrath . . .

It's his voice. His angry laughter. His scorn. His wrath. Just to hear God's voice is to be terrified. What were the nations thinking?

Actually, what is the writer thinking? Because when we eventually hear God speak, his words of terror are a huge anticlimax:

⁶I have installed my king
    on Zion, my holy mountain.

At its greatest historical extent, the kingdom based in Zion exerted various levels of control over seven or eight local kingdoms, but it never once challenged the true world-powers in Egypt and Mesopotamia. And by the time this psalm came to stand over the finished book, there *was* no king in Zion. Judah was a subject people.

The magnificent hyperbole of this verse only makes any sense as a prophecy, a vision of the final judgment alluded to in Psalm 1. The prophecy is based in a promise God made to King David:

> When your days are over and you rest with your ancestors, I will raise up your offspring to succeed you, your own flesh and blood . . . I will establish the throne of his kingdom for ever. I will be his father, and he will be my son.
> (2 Samuel 7:12, 14)

What Psalm 2 does is take God's promise of 'for ever' with complete seriousness. An eternal kingdom has to mean an unconquered kingdom. The fact that the history of Israel turned out to be the history of a failed kingdom puts a tension into the heart of the whole book of Psalms – a tension between God's *promise* and the nation's *experience*. Notice that it's the same tension we saw when Psalm 1 promised prosperity to the righteous person; but here in Psalm 2 we're dealing with the life of an entire nation.

This is the first way in which Psalm 2 fills out the message of Psalm 1. It shows us that the struggles Christ's followers endure as individuals, as families, as church communities, are part of something much bigger. Your decision to walk in Jesus' footsteps catches you up into a drama that stretches across space and time. Psalm 2 shows you that you are not alone.

Gathering to worship in large numbers is an exhilarating physical reminder that we're not alone. Most of us in Australia were deprived of that experience for two years during the coronavirus pandemic. Much of Christ's church in other parts of the world is permanently deprived of that experience. And yet these psalms assure us that we are joined in our walk by a multitude whose allegiance to the LORD binds us together into a great nation.

Scene 3: flashback (2:7–9)

The question remains whether the claims of Psalm 2 can survive the reality of Israel's history. The third scene points us to the answer. The king himself takes over the narration, and invites us to witness the moment, back in the past, when he became king:

> [7]I will proclaim the LORD's decree:
>
> He said to me, 'You are my son;
>   today I have become your father.'

The language used here has been found in the official records of a number of ancient nations, when a king without a clear successor adopted someone as his heir. That's why it's called the LORD's 'decree'. These are legally binding words, and they turn a commoner into a monarch.

The king in this psalm doesn't just inherit the kingdom of Israel. His coronation gift is described in verse 8:

> [8]Ask me, and I will make the nations your inheritance,
>   the ends of the earth your possession.

No sooner does the king receive this gift than he immediately, shockingly, smashes it to pieces:

> [9]You will break them with a rod of iron;
>   you will dash them to pieces like pottery.

It seems a rather reckless thing to do with your inheritance, but the opening scene explains why it's necessary. The son has inherited the world, but it has risen up in rebellion, and has to be smashed before it can be restored.

Remember the first way Psalm 2 completed Psalm 1: it showed us that our faithfulness makes us part of something bigger than ourselves. The second way Psalm 2 completes Psalm 1 is found in the verses we've just read. Psalm 1 simply says, 'The wicked will not stand in the judgment.' Psalm 2 describes that future judgment. It's a description that barely applies to King David, a poetic exaggeration at best. But the Gospels claim that this is the plain and exact truth about David's descendant, Jesus of Nazareth. The validity of that claim rests ultimately on a single event: the resurrection of Jesus from death – the empty tomb, the hundreds of witnesses with whom the risen Christ walked, ate and talked before he ascended to the Father to begin his reign over the nations.

What happened on that first Easter Sunday is both the guarantee and the advance demonstration of the universal smashing of the powers of death that will mark Christ's return. It's a victory in which Christ's people will share, as Christ himself made clear to the church in Thyatira:

> To the one who is victorious and does my will to the end, I will give authority over the nations – that one 'will rule them with an iron sceptre and will dash them to pieces like pottery' – just as I have received authority from my Father.
> (Revelation 2:26–27)

Scene 4: earth (2:10–12)

Psalm 2 ends back on earth in its final scene, with the narrator speaking:

> [10] Therefore, you kings, be wise;
>   be warned, you rulers of the earth.
> [11] Serve the LORD with fear
>   and celebrate his rule with trembling.
> [12] Kiss his son, or he will be angry
>   and your way will lead to your destruction,
> for his wrath can flare up in a moment.
>   Blessed are all who take refuge in him.

God's enemies are warned that in opposing the son they oppose God himself; that if they want to do the smart thing and lay down their arms at God's feet, it will have to be the son's feet they kiss. It's ambiguous in verse 12 who will be angry, the LORD or his son. Most likely it's the LORD, because the final line speaks of taking refuge, and every other time people take refuge in the Psalms, it's always in the LORD. But once again, it's hard to separate them: what's done to the king is done to his Lord.

The choice to oppose the LORD and his king is described in verse 12 using language taken from the end of Psalm 1: 'your way will lead to your destruction.' And this alerts us to a third way in which Psalm 2 completes Psalm 1. The opposition that you face for walking the path of faithfulness is not really directed at you. It's directed at the God who is made visible by your faithfulness. It may not feel like it, but it's a huge compliment.

So there's the drama of Psalm 2. It takes Psalm 1's private world of personal faithfulness and places it onto an international stage. As you strive to walk his way in the face of opposition and discouragement, Psalm 2 assures you of three great truths:

1 You are not alone.
2 Your future has been revealed.
3 The hardships of your faithfulness do you honour.

Travelling in the footsteps of the Messiah

The final words of Psalm 2, 'Blessed are all who take refuge in him', do two things. They point back to the opening word of Psalm 1, and tie the main characters of each psalm together. The person who walks the path more faithfully than any other, whose steps we follow, is also the exalted king who judges God's enemies.

But the words also point forwards. In psalm after psalm the king encourages God's faithful people to take refuge in the LORD (Psalm 5:11 is the first example). But the main refuge-seeker in the

Psalms is the king himself. Perhaps his quiet presence in Psalm 1 should have prepared us for this, but when we hear the king at prayer he sounds nothing like the Messiah of Psalm 2. Ten times in Books I and II he cries out, 'I take refuge! Protect me!'; 'I take refuge! Rescue me!' And many more times he seeks asylum with God without using the language of refuge: desperate, surrounded by enemies too strong to deal with. The tension between appearance and reality that we've already seen a couple of times applies to the king as well. So let's finish this study with two reflections on the character of God's chosen king.

The King's weakness is our weakness

David's weakness is so striking that some scholars think we should see him as a foil to the Messiah, as the failed king who proves our need for God's coming King. But I think that's a mistake. God has always chosen to use weakness to demonstrate his glory. His decision to use the deeply flawed Israelites to bring blessing to the nations is an expression of the same wisdom that gave steward-ship of creation to puny human beings in the first place. As Psalm 8 puts it, God uses the words of infants to bring down the avenging enemy. Our weakness shows his glory. King David is not a foil; he's a key. He shows us that the Messiah of Psalm 2 repre-sents us. He is a human being. He's representative because by himself he is weak. He confesses his weakness with devastating honesty; he casts himself on God's protection; he has no back-up plan.

As the Messiah's people, we are called to be like him in his weakness. Twice in Book I we find the king taking refuge in the LORD, and then encouraging his people to seek refuge as he did (Psalms 18:2, 30; 31:1, 19). For us today, the King whose weakness we imitate is, of course, Jesus the Messiah.

David's journey of weakness, trust and vindication is the same journey Jesus travelled. As the book of Hebrews tells us, Jesus 'offered up prayers and petitions with fervent cries and tears to the one who could save him from death, and he was heard because of his reverent submission' (Hebrews 5:7).

The King's strength is our strength

Did you notice, as we looked at Psalm 2, that the Messiah never acts on his own? In scene 1 the rebels oppose the LORD and his anointed: the two together. In scene 2 the LORD terrifies them by installing his king. In scene 3 they defeat their enemies together: 'I will make', says the LORD, and 'you will break'. And in scene 4 the kings of the earth serve the LORD by kissing the son's feet. In different ways, every scene of this drama draws us in to reflect on the relationship between the LORD and his Messiah, Father and Son.

Most mysteriously of all, in the royal decree of verse 7 we see the father–son relationship coming into existence, as the LORD begets a son and in so doing becomes something he was not – a father. They are both changed – but this is not a change that occurs during the time of the psalm, the time of world history; it is an event the son recalls from an indeterminate past: 'He said to me . . .' It is, in fact, a prophetic depiction of a begetting that took place in the being of God before the beginning, so that there was never a time when there was not a Father and an eternally begotten Son.

But when the LORD installs his king on Zion, it is time for that timeless 'decree' to be *proclaimed*, to be enacted within history. God now has a face, and it is the face of Zion's king. The king now has a voice, and it is the voice of God. This psalm gives us a prophetic portrait of the risen and exalted Lord Jesus, and Jesus is never more royal than when he says in John's Gospel:

> Whatever the Father does the Son also does . . . The Father judges no one, but has entrusted all judgment to the Son, that all may honour the Son just as they honour the Father. Whoever does not honour the Son does not honour the Father, who sent him.
> (John 5:19b, 22–23)

The vision of the king in these opening psalms is both encouraging and emboldening. It encourages us to press on because our King, who is weak, as we are, has endured our troubles already. And it emboldens us in our mission, to set fear aside and to call the nations to recognize the King's victory while there is still time to lay down their arms. The mission of the Psalms is the same mission Paul took up in his sermon to the Athenians:

Repent! Because God has set a day when he will judge the world with justice by the man he has appointed. He has given proof of this to everyone by raising him from the dead. (Acts 17:31, adapted)

2

Psalm 32: weakness and gratitude

Finding a plot in the Psalms

Psalm 2 introduced us to the theme of the book: the universal reign of the LORD and his anointed king. We saw that this theme is worked out in the form of a *plot*: how does the king of Zion come to reign supreme over all the nations?

But it's odd, isn't it, to think of a poetry collection as having a plot. Certainly, the Psalms don't unfold with the narrative orderliness of Genesis or Luke's Gospel. There are some places where a story unfolds across a series of psalms, but more often the connection between a psalm and its neighbours is fairly loose. Everywhere you look, you find a rich patchwork of different types of psalms side by side.

But when you step back, you begin to notice that the patchwork isn't random. For the first half of the book the most common psalms are laments, but as we move towards the end, praise takes over and dominates. And alongside this movement from lament to praise there is a subtler movement through the history of Israel. The life and times of King David dominate Books I and II, Psalms 1 – 72. David is named in the titles of most of these psalms, and many of them have headings that relate to incidents in his life. Psalm 71 is the prayer of an old man who sounds very much like David at the end of his life, and Psalm 72 is a prayer that God would bless the reign of David's son, Solomon.

The backdrop of Book III is the divided kingdom: the 350-year period between Solomon and the exile. All but one of Psalms 73 – 89 are psalms by temple musicians, and all but five are laments, often by the whole community in the face of national disaster. The fall of the northern kingdom is in view in the middle psalms of the book, and by the end the southern kingdom is fallen too. Book III is about the failure of the nation and its kings. It is the low point of the whole book of Psalms.

Despite the fact that Book IV reflects the seventy-year period of exile, things take a turn for the better in Psalms 90 – 106. There is a joyful recognition that the LORD reigns over the nations, and the book ends with a prayer:

> Save us, LORD our God,
>   and gather us from the nations,
> that we may give thanks to your holy name
> (Psalm 106:47)

As Book V opens, we hear that prayer answered:

> Let the redeemed of the LORD tell their story –
>   those he redeemed from the hand of the foe,
> those he gathered from the lands
> (Psalm 107:2–3)

We will look more closely at Books III to V when we come to them; for now it's enough to recognize that the five Books of the Psalms take us through the history of Israel from David to the return from exile. This does not mean that the psalms in each Book were written during that period. It means that the editors of the Psalms often placed psalms in a given Book with a specific period of the nation's history in mind. In this and the next study we are in Books I and II, and we're looking at psalms that mainly concern King David, the untriumphant but faithful messiah who took refuge in God through a life of troubles.

Lament, thanksgiving, praise

Psalm 32 is the central psalm in a cluster of three. The psalm before it is a lament by David as he is overwhelmed by external troubles. Psalm 32 itself is a thanksgiving by David as he is rescued from internal troubles. And Psalm 33 is an anonymous psalm of praise to the Creator and Ruler who saves his chosen nation and its king.

These three psalms cover the three main life-situations we find ourselves in. *Lament* is for the dark times: the sudden crises, or the chronic sorrows. *Praise* is for the bright times: the moments of joy, or the long happy seasons. *Thanksgiving* is for the times of transition from dark to light. As far as our experiences go, only a minority of our lives is taken up by the moments of transition from sorrow to joy. But that transition defines who we are as God's people. As Paul says in Colossians, God 'has rescued us from the dominion of darkness and brought us into the kingdom of the Son he loves' (Colossians 1:13). Thanksgiving for that transition is the fundamental orientation of the Christian, and gospel gratitude shapes the way that we lament and praise as well.

We are going to look at Psalm 32 in two parts. In the first part David makes a bold claim (vv. 1–2): he's found the secret of happiness! He then supports this claim by sharing his backstory (vv. 3–7). In the second part (vv. 8–11) he uses his story to convince us to come and share the secret with him.

Part 1: David's story

Guilt and forgiveness (32:1–2)

Before we begin I want to tell you a story about a powerful man. It begins typically. This man wanted something badly, but someone stood in his way. So he had his rival killed. And because he was so powerful he got away with it. There are plenty of stories like that. But then there's a twist. The man began to feel remorse. And this feeling grew until he was in a state of constant pain.

We can experience unhappiness as a species of physical pain, and different types of physical pain become our reference points for articulating that unhappiness: the sharp pain of betrayal; the chronic ache of grief; the acute agony of remorse. These pains are real, not imagined, and they take their toll on the body just as simple physical pain does.

The sort of pain the man in my story was feeling is the terrible pain of things we've done that we can never undo. The cruel word you can't take back. The act of unfaithfulness that destroys a relationship. The moment of carelessness on the road that takes away a stranger's life. These deeds press down upon our souls with a terrible weight.

Now you may have guessed that the man in my story was King David, who murdered Uriah so he could have his wife. The same man who wrote this psalm. Consider the opening verses:

> ¹Blessed is the one whose transgressions are forgiven,
>   whose sins are covered.
> ²Blessed is the one
>   whose sin the LORD does not count against them
>   and in whose spirit is no deceit.

This is the first use of the word 'blessed' since Psalms 1 and 2. And it adds a new ingredient to our picture of blessedness: the ingredient of pure happiness. For David this happiness began when he was healed of the pain of remorse. Not only remorse for murdering Uriah. That's just scratching the surface.

You'll notice three words for sin in these verses, translated in the NIV as 'transgressions', 'sins', and 'sin' (traditionally translated 'iniquity'). These words are often combined in the Bible to convey the totality of sin. They cover three types of crime.

First, there are the crimes we commit against God and *others*, such as David's murder of Uriah, which was evil in God's sight (2 Samuel 12:9). Second, there are the crimes we commit against God and *self*: crimes labelled with words such as 'impurity' and 'uncleanness'. They may be things done in secret, or even things we are not aware of doing because we are so accustomed to them. And third, there is the crime whose only direct target is *God*, which the Bible labels 'idolatry'. This is the crime of taking the life he gave us and not living it back to him; the crime, fuelled by ingratitude and pride, of setting ourselves up as the gods of our own lives, the choosers of our own path. For people who know God, this least tangible of crimes sits at the very top of the Bible's hierarchy of sin.

Balancing these three words for sin are three descriptions of their removal. The word 'forgiven' contains the image of a burden being lifted away, and it's balanced by the 'covering' in the next line. The complementary images clear a bright space around the poet. His crimes with their terrible consequences, lifted off his shoulders: cleared! The behaviour that disgusts God, covered and removed from sight like a cancer in remission: cleared! These lines of verse 1 are concise labels of identity. This is who I am now: unburdened, unashamed, free to look around and start living.

That's the result of being forgiven. Verse 2 shows us the reason for David's forgiveness. The word for sin here points to crimes so brazen that there was no sacrifice for them in the law of Moses. David had murder and adultery on his conscience. But he has discovered that God's forgiveness does not rely on our crimes somehow being undone, our victims made as good as new. Neither does God require us to be rehabilitated and become new people. We are forgiven only and entirely because 'the Lord does not count sin against us'. The reason for this has nothing to do with us; it is purely and simply an expression of God's character, his glory as he revealed it to Moses in Exodus 34:6. The Lord decides, simply because of who he is – 'the compassionate and gracious God, slow to anger, abounding in love and faithfulness' – to view a sinful human as free of sin, as innocent. He knows what we are far better than we do ourselves. But he decides to lift away the things we have done, to cover over what we are, and to view us unencumbered and clean.

And because it's God doing the lifting and the covering, a miracle happens. What was lifted stays lifted. What was covered stays covered. And we *become* the people he sees when he looks at us.

Forgiveness is the miracle that lies at the heart of the Christian faith. If the gospel of Christ could be reduced to a single word, that word would be 'forgiveness'. If there is one attribute that separates the true and living God from all the gods of every religion that ever there was, that attribute would be forgiveness.

But the last line of verse 2 turns the psalm in a new direction. Alongside this miracle of God's forgiveness, the blessed person is marked by a quality of their own. The person God forgives is no longer animated by *deceitfulness*. The way these two lines are placed together could imply that God took away their deceitfulness along with their other sins. But from the human point of view, the experience of God's forgiveness comes to the one who has dropped all pretence.

David's story (32:3–7)

To explain how this works, David tells us his story. Actually, he tells God his story, as an act of thanksgiving, but he does it in public so we can hear it too. It's a story that unfolds in three stages. We could call stage 1 'the toxic powers of deceit' – of the lies David told himself and God, lies that took the form of silence.

Stage 1: the toxic powers of deceit

Verse 3 combines two long, restless lines that convey a state of terrible pain:

> ³When I kept silent, my bones wasted away
>   through my groaning all day long.

David can no longer live with the things he has done, the people he has hurt, the person he has become, the hypocrisy of his position as role model of God's people. Holding it all in is eating away at him. The word translated 'groaning' usually describes a lion's roar, and though David is not literally roaring here, he is making plenty of noise. His silence is speechlessness, not quietness! David's groans of anguish rise up from deep within him, never stopping, fatiguing his bones as vibrations fatigue the metal in a bridge, until eventually he is worn down, wracked with pain, and brittle as a twig.

We humans will resort to all sorts of tricks to avoid pain like this, tricks the psychologists catalogue under headings such as denial, repression, displacement, projection, rationalization. But in David's case the crushing burden he felt was being pressed down upon him by the hand of God, held in place from dawn to dusk and through the sleepless nights. The image in verse 4 is of the hot sun drying something out until it is completely lifeless: a brown and shrivelled plant, or a dead and desiccated animal:

> ⁴For day and night
>   your hand was heavy on me;
> my strength was sapped
>   as in the heat of summer.

David's silence, his refusal to say out loud what he knows to be true, has pitched him into an experience of intense suffering as God presses the life out of him. No human has the right to treat a fellow human this way. But God has the prerogative, because he and he alone is the LORD, 'abounding in love and faithfulness . . . forgiving wickedness, rebellion and sin' (Exodus 34:6–7). John Newton understood this well when he wrote the lines:

> 'Twas grace that taught my heart to fear,
>   And grace my fears reliev'd.[1]

Stage 2: broken silence, mended life

The second stage of David's testimony is just one verse long (v. 5), ending in the climax, the pivot of the psalm. It is David's moment of re-creation:

> ⁵Then I acknowledged my sin to you
>   and did not cover up my iniquity.
> I said, 'I will confess
>   my transgressions to the LORD.'
> And you forgave
>   the guilt of my sin.

'Blessed is the one . . . whose sins are covered,' said David at the start of the psalm. But before God covers our sins we must uncover them. We must make known to God what God already knows: what we are. David reuses all the words for sin from the opening verses – the crimes committed against God and neighbour; the uncleanness and shame we hide from everyone. God knows it all, but we must tell it all to him anyway. This is not a charade. It's a surrender. A yielding of the will. A confession of helplessness. But it must be spoken; it cannot be held back in painful silence.

The result, when David speaks out, is a definitive act that brings David from the realm of death into light and life: 'You forgave the guilt of my sin.' God's heavy hand lifts, and with it lifts the crushing burden of guilt and condemnation, and David stops dying. He becomes a new person, defined not by his sin and guilt but by its removal. Such a simple thing – break your silence. And such a huge thing at the same time – total surrender. One simple, momentous confession; and then, this miracle! David is looking back on an event in his past, but his awe and gratitude is still fresh. He is telling his story back to God, and the final 'you' of verse 5 is emphatic. 'I broke my silence. Finally. And *you*. Look at what you did.'

I'd like to step out of Psalm 32 for a moment and address you, dear reader. I don't know who you are, and even if I did I would not truly know you. Not as God does. But I want to take a moment to speak specifically to those of you who feel the burden of the things you've done and the person those things have made you, but have never brought that burden to God, never been prepared to make that surrender, that fateful acknowledgment that your life is not yours but his.

If that's you, I want to assure you from long experience that it's safe to place your life in God's hands. It's more than safe; it's liberating and joyful and utterly amazing. You are not forfeiting responsibility or agency or adult choices, because when you give your life to God he makes it new and gives it back again, to live it for him, unburdened and free. To walk a path that will demand all your intelligence and energy and creativity and faithfulness. Your burden is a gift from God, propelling you towards him to find life. And if you are like a hesitant swimmer standing on the beach with your arms wrapped around yourself, this psalm is the person yelling at you from the waves, 'Come on in – the water's great!'

All you need to do is break your silence. Unburden yourself. David explains what this feels like in the third stage of his testimony.

Stage 3: the joy of being forgiven

David is so elated by what God did for him that he wants the rest of us to jump in the water and share in his joy – to pray, right now!

> ⁶Therefore let all the faithful pray to you
> while you may be found;
> surely the rising of the mighty waters
> will not reach them.

He calls us 'faithful' because praying is what faithful people do. If you don't rely on God, you don't pray; and if you don't pray, you don't rely on God. But David doesn't leave it all up to us: he asks God to *make* us prayerful. The second line of verse 6 is a little cryptic, but I don't think that its main purpose is to warn people who delay. It is highlighting the significance of that moment of discovery, that moment when our eyes are opened to who God is, and to what we are as we stand before him. And it's assuring us that the moment when you find God . . . that's *real*. The veil has been removed; we have seen things as they are. And once you've found God, there is nothing left to do but pray.

Being forgiven by God is the pivotal moment of the human life because it changes everything. It lifts the crushing burden of guilt and condemnation, but that's just the start. The purpose of forgiveness is to fill that cleared space with a new relationship. David's crimes had estranged him from God. Then he confessed, he was forgiven, and now he and God are reconciled. They belong together. And that makes David's well-being God's responsibility now.

The 'mighty waters' in the Psalms are an image of the great powers that stand opposed to God and his people. They could be earthly powers, such as hostile kings and nations (as in Psalm 18:16–17), but ultimately they represent the powers of death. The mighty waters are an image full of menace and terror; but David loses interest almost immediately. Why? Because there at the end of his story is God himself, mightier than the waters, but comforting rather than menacing. Verse 7 is an image of real intimacy. An emphatic '*You*' excludes everything but God from the picture:

> ⁷ *You* are my hiding-place;
>   you will protect me from trouble
>   and surround me with songs of deliverance.

The trouble from which God protects David is not only the external trouble of violent enemies and encroaching death. Verse 7 describes the internal troubles that plagued him before he was forgiven. Distress, anxiety, inner torment. God's forgiveness broke down the walls of turmoil he built up around himself, and replaced them with walls of song. This is a unique image as far as I know, and it describes the core identity and posture of the forgiven.

David and Jesus

Before we reflect on how this psalm speaks to us as Christ's people, we need to tackle a sticky problem of interpretation. It's all very well to say, as I did in the previous study, that King David foreshadows Messiah Jesus in his humanity, and that David's prayers belong to Jesus before they belong to us. But how can this be true when David confesses his sin, given that Jesus had no sins to confess? Was David only sometimes a model of the Christ to come?

The beginning of the answer to this question can be found in 2 Samuel 23:

> These are the last words of David:
>
> 'The inspired utterance of David son of Jesse,
>   the utterance of the man exalted by the Most High,
> the man anointed by the God of Jacob,
>   the hero of Israel's songs:
>
> The Spirit of the LORD spoke through me;
>   his word was on my tongue.'
> (2 Samuel 23:1–2)

The psalms of David are not just poetry; they are also prophecy. And the prophet to whom God spoke was David. So what does it mean for David to be a prophet? It means being called to stand between God and Israel, like Moses before him. And from that position David does two things. As God's representative he speaks the word of God to the people. And as the people's representative he speaks the people's words to God.

So when King David confessed his sins, he was not just confessing his own sins. Speaking as a prophet he was confessing on behalf of the nation as well. What set David apart from the nation was the deep regret, sorrow and humility that David felt when he sinned. The prayer he prays in this psalm is the prayer all the people of Israel desperately needed to pray, but which in the end they chose not to. It is a model of repentance that stands before them in written form as the prophetic word of God.

Unlike David, Jesus was not guilty of any sin. And yet he was sent into the world to represent God to the people and to represent the people to God. He was baptized for sins he did not commit. He led his disciples in praying 'Forgive us our sins', and he died condemned for sins he alone was not guilty of. His whole life was representative, and in that sense David's prayers are his as well.

When Jesus attended the synagogue at Nazareth, I don't think he stopped singing when the congregation got to Psalm 32. But he did not sing about his own sins. He sang as the representative of Israel and indeed of the world, suffering the pain of our stubborn silence and feeling God's hand heavy upon him, confessing our sins, which he took upon himself and bore as his own crushing burden. And because of his perfect obedience he was lifted up by a word of power, a word that when it is spoken to us says, 'You are forgiven.'

As we hear the voice of Christ in this psalm, we come to verse 6 and see it in a new light. First of all, we hear Jesus inviting us to join him in drawing near to the Father to find life and safety. And then the cryptic second line, 'while you may be found', points to the time in history when God became findable in a new way, when his goodness and power were put on display for all to see. If you are someone who feels the hand of God on your life at this moment, calling you to come clean and come home, this line is pointing you to the cross of Christ, and inviting you to direct your confession to the Lord Jesus.

Part 2: living the forgiven life

The wisdom of the forgiven person (32:8–10)

In the last part of this psalm we see two changes in the life of the forgiven king, and they apply to all forgiven people. First, the forgiven person becomes *teachable*. Verse 8 is a word from God to the king, which he then passes on to his people:

> ⁸I will instruct you and teach you in the way you should go;
>   I will counsel you with my loving eye on you.

What God spoke to Israel through David he now speaks to the church through Christ Jesus, and that makes these verses a model for our own experience of forgiveness. Having tasted the joys of forgiveness, our hearts become open to God and we gain an appetite for his teaching. The 'way' in verse 8 is the same way, or path, that the blessed person walks in Psalm 1. Once we've been forgiven we are God's, and he keeps us on track.

Second, the forgiven person becomes *a teacher*. In verse 9 David turns his experience of remaining silent into a proverb:

> ⁹Do not be like the horse or the mule,
>   which have no understanding
> but must be controlled by bit and bridle
>   or they will not come to you.

'Don't be stupid like I was,' David is advising us. 'See how much pain I had to suffer before I finally came to God. If I'd known then what I know now, I could have spared myself all that.'

In verse 10 David then does the same with his experience of forgiveness, creating a second proverb for our consideration:

[10]Many are the woes of the wicked,
  but the LORD's unfailing love
  surrounds the one who trusts in him.

The 'woes of the wicked' means their pain and suffering – pain that is healed by trust, as David found in verse 5. And what is the experience of the person who trusts God? His unfailing love surrounds you. *Can I be sure? After all, it's a big step.* Yes, says David, you can be sure. He goes back to his experience of being surrounded by a wall of song (v. 7), and uses it to create a second image of enclosure. God's unfailing love forms a wall of safety between the forgiven person and the woes of the wicked, the pains of death. God's love is the security of the forgiven person.

To walk through life in the embrace of God's love does not mean living free from trouble or care or sorrow or hardship. Just think of the life of Jesus. But it does mean being kept secure through every hardship, sustained through every season by God's unfailing love, until finally we are kept secure through the mighty waters of death and brought by the power of his forgiveness into life imperishable, when we will be like Christ because we will see him as he is (1 John 3:2).

The joy of the forgiven person (32:11)

David's final instruction for the forgiven person is simple:

[11]Rejoice in the LORD and be glad, you righteous;
  sing, all you who are upright in heart!

Rejoice! Not in your blessings and good fortune, but in the LORD. There is never a time in your life, be it ever so difficult, when you cannot remind yourself of what God has done for you, and let him be the wellspring of your thankfulness. There is no attack so devastating, no loss so severe, that it can take away from you the greatest treasure you could ever have: you are forgiven.

In John Bunyan's tale *The Pilgrim's Progress*, there is a lovely moment after Christian comes to the cross and feels his burden roll off his shoulders into the grave. First he weeps in relief and amazement. And then, writes Bunyan:

Christian gave three leaps for joy, and went on singing:

'Thus far I did come laden with my sin;
Nor could aught ease the grief that I was in.
Till I came hither: What a place is this!
Must here be the beginning of my bliss?
Must here the burden fall from off my back?
Must here the strings that bound it to me crack?
Blest cross! blest sepulchre! blest rather be
The man that there was put to shame for me!'[2]

Forgiveness and the Christian life

I want to finish by reflecting on the significance of the joy of forgiveness for the life of the church and for the work of mission.

The rhythm of the Christian life

The rhythm of confession, forgiveness and thanksgiving is the rhythm of the Christian life. In Psalm 32:10 the opposite of wickedness is not goodness, but trust. The faithful person, the godly person, is the one who prays for forgiveness. In Psalm 18, David – David the murderer – says something that should take your breath away:

The LORD has dealt with me according to my righteousness;
    according to the cleanness of my hands he has rewarded
        me.
For I have kept the ways of the LORD;
    I am not guilty of turning from my God.
(Psalm 18:20–21)

How can he say this?! He can say it because the opposite of wickedness is trust. His humble and heartfelt turning back to God in confession has been met by a love that does not count his sin against him. And

David knows this is no legal fiction. He stands before God clean, whole and righteous.

God's act of forgiveness through Christ is world-changing and world-spanning. Its powers reach out from the cross to touch every point in space and time. But once God calls us into relationship with him, we *exercise* that relationship by availing ourselves of his forgiveness whenever we become conscious of sin.

Confession is the great antidote to pride, hypocrisy and self-deception. We wish it didn't have to be this way, and we know that one day it won't, but in the meantime the sin that clings to our souls turns our lives into a series of gospel moments, and places thanksgiving at the heart of what it means to walk the Christian path.

If you are young, let me break it to you. You will never reach a point in your Christian walk where you do not need to confess your sins to God. Augustine of Hippo, one of the greatest Fathers of the Church, had Psalm 32 written on the wall by his sickbed as he lay dying. With this psalm in mind he wrote, 'The beginning of knowledge is to know oneself a sinner.'[3]

Do not neglect corporate confession

The book of Psalms was the prayerbook of Israel. And in verse 6 David models confession not just for the private reader but also for the gathered congregation. If you are an Anglican you may know these words from the Order for Morning and Evening Prayer:

> The Scriptures urge us to acknowledge our many sins, and not to conceal them in the presence of God our heavenly Father; but to confess them with a penitent and obedient heart, so that we may be forgiven through his boundless goodness and mercy.
> We ought always humbly to admit our sins before God; but especially when we assemble and meet together.[4]

The Prayer Book speaks of *general* confession, because the place for specific and detailed confession is at home. When we confess our sins together, we confess generically to honour the body of Christ by not airing the unedifying particulars of our lives; and we confess generically to honour Christ himself, by ensuring that our sins are not the hero but, rather, God the forgiver. Very thankfully, God doesn't work by forgiving the sins you remember to name. When you pray honestly and sincerely, God hears and forgives *you*, the person.

There are three reasons why sin should 'especially' be confessed together:

1 To confess your sins out loud in the presence of others has a moral seriousness that private confession lacks. It's a public confession of faith, not just sin, and it strengthens us precisely by its public nature.
2 We don't sin just as individuals; we also sin as a community. As the person next to you hears you confess, she may remember your sin against her, and perhaps even be emboldened to talk to you about it. As the pastor hears his congregation confessing, it should shape the way he addresses the sin we commit together, as a community.
3 General confession enables general absolution. The Anglican Prayer Book gives the task of declaring forgiveness to a minister, but not because they are doling out forgiveness from some mystical stash they got from being ordained! The minister gets the job because he or she is qualified to preach the gospel. When I say 'Almighty God pardon you', I'm not praying that God might; I'm declaring, as Christ's ambassador, that he has.

Being forgiven empowers us to forgive others

The topic of forgiving others is too large and important to be tacked on as an appendix to a psalm about God forgiving us. Let me just say that God's forgiveness is absolutely fundamental to any discussion about forgiveness between people. We know how deep the rifts can be that sin creates between us, and how difficult it can be to achieve restitution, forgiveness and reconciliation. But the deepest of all rifts is the one made between us and God. If God holds a crime against you, it doesn't matter how well you atone for it in the human sphere. And if God lifts the burden of guilt from you, then another person's refusal to forgive you is painful but not fatal. Best of all, being unburdened by God frees us to offer his forgiveness (and our own) to others. But as I say, that's another story.

The message of forgiveness is the heart of the gospel

The idea of Christian mission is deeply offensive to secular society in the twenty-first century. But as Christ's followers we insist, as he did, that the world needs the gospel above all things, and that there is no greater gift we can share with anyone. This gift, as Psalm 32 has shown us, amounts to a single word: forgiveness. The theologian Karl Barth puts it like this:

> Is there not in the Christian faith yet something other than forgiveness of sins? It should be noticed that the Apostles' Creed, speaking of Christian life in the present time, mentions only the forgiveness of sins. Luther and Calvin did the same, they who essentially put forth one truth alone: the forgiveness of sins, which they used then to call justification by faith. Were they right in thus narrowing down all Christianity, all the Christian life and faith to one single point? I think the answer should be: Yes, the Creed and the Reformers were right. For the forgiveness of sins is the basis, the sum, the criterion, of all that may be called Christian life or faith.[5]

The joy of forgiveness is the engine of mission

Finally, and for me most powerfully, this psalm brings to life the overwhelming joy of knowing that you are forgiven, of feeling your burden roll off your shoulders, your shame covered, your sin no longer counted against you. And, as the second half of this psalm models for us, thankfulness for forgiveness is the engine of mission. The evangelist is most fundamentally a person who knows what it is to be forgiven, and who just wants to share that joy with everyone.

I want to finish by sharing some words that beautifully capture the dynamic of the Christian life, from forgiveness to mission. They were spoken by Isaiah:

In that day you will say:

'I will praise you, LORD.
　　Although you were angry with me,
your anger has turned away
　　and you have comforted me.
Surely God is my salvation;
　　I will trust and not be afraid.
The LORD, the LORD himself, is my strength
　　　　and my defence;
　　he has become my salvation.'
With joy you will draw water
　　from the wells of salvation.

In that day you will say:

'Give praise to the LORD, proclaim his name;
　　make known among the nations what he has done,
　　and proclaim that his name is exalted.
Sing to the LORD, for he has done glorious things;
　　let this be known to all the world.'
(Isaiah 12:1–5)

3
Psalm 69:
suffering and hope

The Psalms as prophecy

As we continue thinking about the Psalms as a book, I'm going to press 'pause' on the plot. Instead I want to say something more about why we might link the psalms in Books I and II with the life of David.

On the one hand, the answer is simple. Psalm 72:20 identifies all the preceding psalms as 'the prayers of David son of Jesse'. Most of the psalms in Books I and II are headed, 'Of David', and the natural meaning of that heading is a psalm *by* David, a psalm he wrote or performed. The seven psalms in Book II headed 'of Asaph' or 'of the Sons of Korah' are not by David, but they are 'of David' in the sense that they are *about* him. (A single psalm headed 'of David' – Psalm 20 – is about David, and Augustine, for one, took it to mean 'concerning David'.[1])

On the other hand, Davidic psalms sometimes seem to relate to times long after David died. For example, Psalm 69 speaks of saving Zion and rebuilding the cities of Judah, which sounds more like the exile. It's not impossible that it describes a crisis during David's reign, but from earliest times there were devout readers (I'm thinking of the authors of the Jewish Targums and the Church Father Theodoret) who took this psalm as referring to the exile.[2]

Now the Psalms were sung throughout Israel's long history, and perhaps extra verses were added under the inspiration of the Spirit to apply Psalm 69 to new situations. We simply don't know. The early scholars I just mentioned assumed these verses were prophecies by David. They may be right. What we do know is that the psalms which first belonged to David were handed over to the nation after his death, to represent the experiences of later generations. Details that were true of David often turn out to be prophetically true – sometimes truer – of kings and prophets after him. But the life of David never stops being a lens through which we appreciate their ultimate meaning and significance, especially in the first seventy-two psalms.

Psalm 69 is one of the 'Big Five'. It shares top spot with Psalms 2, 22, 110 and 118 as the psalms used most frequently by the apostles to understand the person and work of the Lord Jesus. And if we are going to deepen our understanding of Jesus through Psalm 69, it helps to appreciate that it was already functioning as fulfilled prophecy before Jesus was born. Yes, we can read parts of David's life story in the psalm if we try: his zeal for the temple that led him to move the ark of the covenant into Jerusalem at great cost; the enemies such as Shimei who taunted and abused him when Absalom drove him from power. But the Old Testament person this psalm fits best is the prophet Jeremiah. Psalm 69 prophesied of him before it prophesied of Jesus.

So as we study this lament together, I won't often refer to 'the psalmist', or 'David'. I will mostly say 'the prophet', meaning David in the first instance, but pointing beyond him to the experiences of Jeremiah and, ultimately, Jesus. First, however, I'd like to say a word about what lament is, and how to do it.

The art of lament

What is lament?

The simplest description of biblical lament I can think of is this: *the response of faith to an experience of death.* God's people lament when death, in one form or another, extends its tendrils into our lives. Serious illness is the most obvious example. We don't often think about relationship troubles in terms of death, unless they are extreme, such as losing access to your children through a bad divorce, or losing your place in society after being publicly convicted or cancelled or shamed. But even in less extreme cases, erosion of relationship is erosion of life. As humans, our sense of who we are comes from relationships. In the sphere of family I am a husband, a father, an uncle, a son. You may be a daughter, a wife, a mother. In the sphere of the community I am an employee, a workmate, a friend. In the sphere of society I am a taxpayer, a voter. I'm a church member and a partner in mission. And just as I am a step closer to death when one of my body systems fails, so also when one of my relational systems goes down.

In the Psalms, as in most cultures today, to lose your place in human society is to lose who you are, and therefore to die. To fall into the pit. To be alone in the dark. But that's not the worst thing. Worst of all, if we are humans because God remembers and knows us, then to be forgotten by God is the ultimate cancellation, the ultimate loss of self.

To the secular mind, death just happens to be the way things are. To complain about a property of the universe is as illogical as it is natural. But we know that life was not meant to be this way. Whenever death encroaches on God's people, in whatever form, the faithful response is lament. Lament is not about self-pity. Laments are urgent prayers, appeals to the One who has promised to put an end to suffering and death. They are models of prayer that our churches have largely lost, but we still need them as much as ever.

A dummy's guide to writing lament

Typically, a lament has three steps. Step 1 involves yelling 'Help!' and describing our troubles to God. In step 2 we remember who God is: his power as Creator and his love as Redeemer. We boldly choose to trust that God will *be* that God to us, and we ask him to bring us from death back into life. In step 3 we imagine a day – perhaps a far distant day – when God hears our prayer and fills us with praise once again.

We can boil those three steps down to three actions involving the present, the past and the future: *describe* your predicament; *remember* who God is and entrust your requests to that God; *imagine* how you will praise God when he hears you.

Three sources of death

We have our three steps, but how do we get started? Remember that lament is a response to an experience of death, whether that's something we feel *internally*, such as pain; or *socially*, such as hostility; or *theologically*, such as God's absence.[3] And it's very common, when psalmists describe their troubles in step 1, for them to lament in all three directions. Psalm 13, for example, opens with two lines of God-lament, followed by two lines of self-lament and finally a line of enemy-lament:

> How long, LORD? Will you forget me for ever?
>   How long will you hide your face from me?
> How long must I wrestle with my thoughts
>   and day after day have sorrow in my heart?
>   How long will my enemy triumph over me?
> (Psalm 13:1–2)

Psalm 80:4–6 is an example of a whole community lamenting in the same three directions. Every psalm does it differently, but being aware of these three sources of death can often help us discern the flow of the poet's thought.

The structure of Psalm 69

This is the longest psalm we will look at, so we will examine it in larger sections than usual. First of all, though, it's helpful to see how the whole thing hangs together as it moves through the three steps of lament (see Figure 3).

STEP 1		STEP 2 (cont.)	
1	**Save** me!	13b	Answer me with **salvation**!
5	You know, God	19	You know, God
		29	May your **salvation** protect me
STEP 2		**STEP 3**	
13a	As for me, I pray	30	As for me, I will praise
		35	God will **save** Zion

Figure 3 **Clues to the structure of Psalm 69**

There are three features that point to the psalm's structure:

1 There is an emphatic 'I' in verses 13 and 30. This word marks the transitions between the three steps of the lament.
2 'You know', in verses 5 and 19, divides the first two steps into two halves each.
3 The psalm's opening cry, 'Save me!', is referenced three times in steps 2 and 3, and ties the whole psalm together. If you want a theme word for Psalm 69 you could do worse than 'salvation'.

Step 1: the cry for help

Self-lament and enemy-lament (69:1–4)

Salvation in the Old Testament is basically a physical concept. God saves helpless people from violent death at the hands of ruthless enemies. Not that salvation from sin is any different, of course. There may be no immediate physical violence involved, but the end result of sin is the physical destruction of our bodies. The Psalms can help keep us from overspiritualizing the idea of salvation, starting with the self-lament of these opening verses:

> [1]Save me, O God,
>> for the waters have come up to my neck.
> [2]I sink in the miry depths,
>> where there is no foothold.
> I have come into the deep waters;
>> the floods engulf me.
> [3]I am worn out calling for help;
>> my throat is parched.
> My eyes fail,
>> looking for my God.
> [4]Those who hate me without reason
>> outnumber the hairs of my head;
> many are my enemies without cause,
>> those who seek to destroy me.

I am forced to restore
what I did not steal.

If we were to say 'The water's up to my neck' today, we would probably mean we are busy but coping. But for the prophet, his neck is the bit of him that lets the breath of life into his body, and that life is in immediate danger from chaotic forces. As he tries to convey just what he is going through, he assembles a collection of poetic words for deep water in which a person can't swim: water that drags down; water that traps the feet; water that has no bottom; water that floods over. It reminds me of a horrifying sequence in a film from more than twenty years ago in which a character falls one night into a swimming pool with a plastic cover, which wraps and tangles him as he sinks struggling into the dark water, unable to draw breath.[4]

'This is how I feel,' the prophet tells God, even though God already knows. God already knows, but the prophet has been calling for help to the point where he has no voice left to call with.

Verse 3 is a new image, just as vivid, of a person calling out in desperation and then looking so intently for signs of help that he can't focus any more. Like treading on a bear trap in the woods and calling out through the cold night as you feel yourself weakening, staring at the horizon so hard that you don't know if it's torchlight you see or a hallucination. 'I'm here!' he yells at God, even though God sees him.

Only then does the psalmist speak about the enemies who have brought him so much suffering. Each line in verse 4 builds on the one before. His enemies are numerous; their hatred is gratuitous; their power is overwhelming; they're impervious to truth or argument. What they have actually done to him is delayed to the end of the verse, and left vague. Probably they are opposing him in court, corrupting justice so they can defraud him with the backing of the state. But it's the impact of this *on* him that he mainly sets before God. He's being destroyed socially and relationally, by people who can no more be argued with than floodwaters. They don't want justice or truth. Behind a veil of argument and due process they just want to see him suffer, and they have the numbers and the influence to crush him until there's nothing left.

God knows all this. But when you lament you tell him anyway. That's how a relationship works.

God-lament? (69:5–6)

Now at this point we would often find a God-lament: 'Why are you so far from me? How long will you turn away from me?' But here is where Psalm 69 starts to become something special:

> ⁵You, God, know my folly;
>   my guilt is not hidden from you.
>
> ⁶Lord, the LORD Almighty,
>   may those who hope in you
>   not be disgraced because of me;
> God of Israel,
>   may those who seek you
>   not be put to shame because of me.

There's been an uncomfortable truth rising to the surface of this psalm, and now we see it emerge. Everything that's happened to this poor man has happened under the watchful gaze of a God who knows the hearts of everyone involved, who knows the rights and wrongs of the situation as no-one else does, who knows that the psalmist doesn't deserve his suffering . . . and who yet does nothing.

'My guilt is not hidden from you' is not a confession that the prophet is to blame. It's pointing out a contrast between God, who knows his folly, and his enemies, from whom his guilt *is* hidden. If he'd lost his temper in court and lashed out without thinking, that would be an act of folly his enemies could see and exploit. But the fact is, although he's a sinner, he does not deserve what's happening to him.

What the prophet is doing here is actually very impressive. In the midst of his victimization he takes a moment to self-reflect, to subject himself to God's judgment and to give up the moral superiority he had every right to feel.

And then, just as impressively, in verse 6 he reaches beyond the isolation of his persecution to think of others who will go down with him if he sinks. 'If you allow me to be swallowed up in death,' he says to God, 'others who hope in you as I do will be publicly shamed and humiliated.'

And that won't just be a disaster for them. The climax of each line of verse 6 is its description of God, which gets a whole line of poetry to itself each time. 'LORD Almighty' points to God's power to overcome every other power. 'God of Israel' points to God's special commitment to his people. The existence of *this* God is on the line. Why on earth would God allow that? Consider the facts. He knows every thought of every heart. He knows David's innocence. He knows the impact David's destruction would have on other believers. He could easily intervene if he chose to, and, what's more, he promised he would. But despite all that, God chooses to let David's terrible suffering drag on, even though it drags God's own name down into the mud with him.

But at this point I want to stop thinking about David and start thinking about Jeremiah.

Introducing Jeremiah

Jeremiah lived in the dying days of the nation of Judah, when the rich and powerful used to abuse the poor and then go to the temple and sacrifice tokens of their ill-gotten gain to keep themselves on God's good side. They knew all about God's promise to Abraham to bless his descendants, and they reckoned that they could get away with anything because God would have to forgive them.

So God sent Jeremiah, filled with God's own wrath and sorrow, to speak his wrath and sorrow over them. Jeremiah stood inside the temple gates and preached these words at the pious worshippers:

> Will you steal and murder, commit adultery and perjury, burn incense to Baal and follow other gods you have not known, and then come and stand before me in this house, which bears my

name, and say 'We are safe' – safe to do all these detestable
things? ... The LORD has rejected and abandoned this generation that is under his wrath.
(Jeremiah 7:9, 29)

How did Jeremiah himself react to those fiery words? Here's a little
sample:

Since my people are crushed, I am crushed:
    I mourn, and horror grips me.
Is there no balm in Gilead?
    Is there no physician there?
Why then is there no healing
    for the wound of my people?
(Jeremiah 8:21–22)

Jeremiah was a member of the generation under God's wrath. But
the anguish he felt about the people's sin was not just his own
anguish as an Israelite. It was God's sorrow as well, a sorrow God
gave the prophet so that the people would see how God felt about
destroying them.

And how did Jeremiah's listeners react? Not surprisingly, they
hated him for it. But of course it was really God they hated, because
it was God's wrath and God's sorrow they were reacting against.
Jeremiah's own family plotted to kill him. His society shunned
him. He was placed on trial for predicting the destruction of the
temple.

The mystery of God's inaction (69:7–12)

The story of Jeremiah makes it easy for us to grasp the prophet's
complaint about God's inaction in verses 7–12:

⁷For I endure scorn for your sake,
    and shame covers my face.
⁸I am a foreigner to my own family,
    a stranger to my own mother's children;

⁹for zeal for your house consumes me,
  and the insults of those who insult you fall on me.
¹⁰When I weep and fast,
  I must endure scorn;
¹¹when I put on sackcloth,
  people make sport of me.
¹²Those who sit at the gate mock me,
  and I am the song of the drunkards.

Each of these lines opens a window into the mind of a prophet whose churning thoughts we can almost hear:

'I endure scorn for your sake.' *Because you want me to. When I'm attacked by evil people I don't stop trusting in you. I don't resort to corruption, to violence, to lies. I fight back with prayer. With truth. And you let me lose. So I get scorned, and so covered with shame that when my family look at me they don't see me any more. They just see the shame, and they don't want to know me. And I put up with it, for your sake. As your representative. What on earth are they supposed to learn about you from seeing me like this?*

'Zeal for your house consumes me.' *We're on the same side, LORD. I know what they've done. I know that judgment is coming, and so I do all the things that they* aren't *doing, in the hope that it might make a difference. I pray for forgiveness, I fast and I mourn that you might stay your hand. And what do I get for it?*

'Those who sit at the gate mock me.' *The people who run the show, the elders, the judges. They find the sight of me repenting for their sins incredibly offensive, which is hardly surprising. But you know that they only attack me because when they look at me they see you, and they hate what they see.*

  Sure, I get it! You are using my pain to strip away the veneer of their religiosity, to bring their hidden hatred to the surface, to make them ripe for judgment. But I can't bear the pain! And I can't see why I have to. Destroying your own people is not who you are, God of Israel.

48

Letting your representative die does not show anybody that you are LORD Almighty! This is not the ending you gave Abraham when you told him to look up at the stars. Please, Lord, I beg you. Make this all stop!

And so Jeremiah, foreshadowing Jesus, prays for a time of God's favour. For a time when the insults and the shame come to an end. For a day of resurrection. Step 2 of his lament begins in verse 13.

Step 2: the prayer for salvation

Rescue for the prophet? (69:13–18)

The prophet's prayer for a time of favour is not just a cry of desperation. Sometimes when we find ourselves in a sudden crisis, we shoot off prayers that come out of our fear: 'Please God, let me find the phone I left on the train. Let someone hand it in.' But when you lament, you discipline yourself to step back from your trouble and reflect on the character of the God you are praying to:

> ¹³ But I pray to you, LORD,
>   in the time of your favour;
> in your great love, O God,
>   answer me with your sure salvation.
> ¹⁴Rescue me from the mire,
>   do not let me sink;
> deliver me from those who hate me,
>   from the deep waters.
> ¹⁵Do not let the floodwaters engulf me
>   or the depths swallow me up
>   or the pit close its mouth over me.
>
> ¹⁶Answer me, LORD, out of the goodness of your love;
>   in your great mercy turn to me.
> ¹⁷Do not hide your face from your servant;
>   answer me quickly, for I am in trouble.

¹⁸Come near and rescue me;
  deliver me because of my foes.

In verse 13 the prophet identifies two of the core attributes of Israel's God: his *love*, which is the deep concern and exclusive affection he reserves for his covenant people; and the *sureness* with which he saves, his utter reliability and faithfulness. The prophet hardly mentions his enemies at all. Instead, he summons up the character of God, the love that lies at the deepest core of his being, and brings that God into his terrible feelings from verses 1 and 2 of being surrounded by death.

While Jerusalem was being besieged by the Babylonians, the city officials managed to find some time to bring Jeremiah to the king and ask for him to be put to death for discouraging everyone. The king said 'Sure, go for it', so, as Jeremiah 38 reports, 'They lowered Jeremiah by ropes into a cistern; it had no water in it, only mud, and Jeremiah sank down into the mire' (Jeremiah 38:6, adapted).

The prophet who pleads for rescue from the mire in Psalm 69:14 ends his description with a new image in verse 15: the pit closing its mouth over him. This is an image of death. It's the first time he has said that he thinks he might actually die. And so he returns to the character of the LORD, in verse 16. He repeats the word 'love', but adds a new attribute: 'mercy'. This is a deep compassion for the helpless, like the feelings of a mother for her young child.

God is terribly absent. None of the prophet's prayers have been heard. And now that death is approaching, seven cries for help cascade out of him in just three verses: *Answer me! Turn to me! Don't hide from me! Answer me! Come near to me! Rescue me! Deliver me! Please, God, be like a mother who suddenly senses her child is in trouble and races out, heart beating, to the street.*

Judgment for the prophet's enemies (69:19–28)

But instead of getting better, things only get worse. The prophet's enemies come back into the frame in verses 19–21, and they have come to finish him off. He is so traumatized and close to death that he's completely helpless, so they come visiting with a meal from the church freezer, except they've laced it with poison. He begged for God to come running like an anxious mother, but instead he got the mouth of the pit:

> 19You know how I am scorned, disgraced and shamed;
>   all my enemies are before you.
> 20Scorn has broken my heart
>   and has left me helpless;
> I looked for sympathy, but there was none,
>   for comforters, but I found none.
> 21They put gall in my food
>   and gave me vinegar for my thirst.

So far I've been reading this psalm with Jeremiah in mind as its first fulfilment. There is more of his life in this psalm, but we must pass over it, because it's time to take the next step and think about Jesus. Everything we've read so far describes the life of Jesus just as precisely as it describes Jeremiah. But with verse 21 we begin to move beyond Jeremiah. It's a verse we know Jesus was thinking about as he hung dying:

> Later, knowing that everything had now been finished, and *so that Scripture would be fulfilled*, Jesus said, 'I am thirsty.' A jar of wine vinegar was there, so they soaked a sponge in it, put the sponge on a stalk of the hyssop plant, and lifted it to Jesus' lips. (John 19:28–29)

Jeremiah's prayer in Psalm 69, grounded in an appeal to God's love and compassion, was answered by a persecution so severe that he felt he would die. When Jesus actually *is* killed, the question of what happened to the God of love becomes all the more acute. We'll put a bookmark in that question to come back to it.

First we have to deal with another question, and that's the question raised by verses 22–28:

> 22May the table set before them become a snare;
>   may it become retribution and a trap.

[23] May their eyes be darkened so they cannot see,
    and their backs be bent for ever.
[24] Pour out your wrath on them;
    let your fierce anger overtake them.
[25] May their place be deserted;
    let there be no one to dwell in their tents.
[26] For they persecute those you wound
    and talk about the pain of those you hurt.
[27] Charge them with crime upon crime;
    do not let them share in your salvation.
[28] May they be blotted out of the book of life
    and not be listed with the righteous.

[29] But as for me, afflicted and in pain –
    may your salvation, God, protect me.

These are confronting and difficult verses, and Christians have always struggled to know what to do with prayers like this. They certainly don't feel very 'Christian', so to speak, and most of us feel acutely uncomfortable saying them. To imagine Jesus saying them, as I think we must, is even more troubling. How could the man who prayed, 'Father, forgive them, for they do not know what they are doing' (Luke 23:34), pray something like this?

To answer this question we have to clarify what the prophet's enemies have done; what he is asking God to do to them; and why.

1 What have they done? Verses 20–21: they have drawn him in with a pretence of fellowship so they can betray and wound him all over again, and they've done it with cruel joy.

2 What does the prophet pray for? He starts out by asking that they would feel the effects of their own behaviour. Verse 22: May the treachery they unleash on me at the dinner table rebound and trap them instead. Verse 23: May the eyes they use to carry out their plans, and the backs that give them fighting strength, be prevented from acting.

But then in verses 24–25 he asks for more: Don't just stop them from killing me. Bring upon them the wrath that you reserve for rebellious Israel, which leaves the whole land empty and uninhabited.

And finally comes the really challenging prayer, in verses 27–28, for them to suffer eternal death and condemnation. That's not something any of us would pray for our worst enemy. So why is it in this psalm?

3 Why does the prophet pray like this? The key is verse 26:

> For they persecute those you wound
>   and talk about the pain of those you hurt.

We've seen what it looks like for a prophet to be wounded by God. It looks like coming to the people bearing God's wrath and sorrow for their sins, and being reviled for it because of the people's hatred of God. The insults of people who insult God fall on God's prophet. And God chooses not to save his prophet, despite his desperate cries for help. Instead, God waits to see if the people who set out to kill him will have a moment of regret. And what happens? They draw near to God's dying messenger, and they finish him off, and they boast about it.

Verse 26 is talking about people who know God has come among them, who know that he demands their repentance and obedience, but who decide to kill him instead. These are not the people Jesus prayed for on the cross – the Roman soldiers who crucified him and divided up his clothes. These are the people who *did* know what they were doing – the people who plotted Jesus' death in full awareness that he was sent by God. In Luke 13:34–35 Jesus quotes from this passage when he laments over Jerusalem: 'You who kill the prophets ... Look, your house is left to you desolate' (see Psalm 69:25). In Acts 1:20 Peter quotes the same verse in reference to Judas Iscariot. In Romans 11:9 Paul quotes from this passage to illustrate the hardening of Israel.

The closing appeal for salvation in verse 29 is tied tightly to the preceding verses by its opening, 'But as for me ...' It reveals a prophetic awareness that the salvation of God's prophet depends on the final destruction of God's enemies. Jesus must die not only to secure the salvation of those who trust in him but also to secure the judgment of those who will not.

What it was like for Jesus to be Jesus

Psalm 69 sheds a prophetic light on the suffering that God embraced at his incarnation. Like Jeremiah, Jesus was rejected by his family, consumed by zeal for the LORD's house, hated without reason and condemned to death in a corrupt court by the lies of evil men.

No doubt Psalm 69 helped Jesus to interpret his own life – given over to death; aware that his obedience would only accelerate Israel's rejection of God and the plot to kill him; willing for God's wrath against his people to fall in the first place upon its one faithful member; but overwhelmed with distress that the price he must pay was so terrible.

The final twist of the knife in verse 21 points to the intensification of Jesus' suffering in the last week of his life. But the first twelve verses of the psalm give us an insight into the whole of Jesus' life. Jesus came as God's representative, filled with God's own anger and grief in the face of Israel's wanton rebellion. At the same time, he lived as Israel's representative, enduring the people's growing hostility with perfect godliness, offering up the tearful prayers and petitions they failed to offer. Jesus did not begin to suffer only in Gethsemane. Not a moment of his earthly ministry was untroubled. It was crushingly difficult just to be who he was. We need psalms like this to nurture our gratitude and love.

What did all that suffering achieve? We know that it taught him obedience and made him the perfect saviour for all who obey him. But Psalm 69 teaches us that it was also the price Jesus paid to secure the judgment of all whose hearts are implacably hostile towards their God, together with all the forces of evil and death.

But the judgment of God's enemies, a judgment that brings Jesus' suffering to an end, is not the last word. In step 3 of the psalm, the prophet reaches around his suffering and God's silence, and grabs tight hold of the Saviour he knows God to be.

Step 3: the praise of David's God

The risen King (69:30–31)

In the final stage of his lament, the prophet – we'll call him Jesus – imagines the day he will experience God as Saviour:

> ³⁰I will praise God's name in song
>   and glorify him with thanksgiving.
> ³¹This will please the LORD more than an ox,
>   more than a bull with its horns and hooves.

There was nothing wrong with animal sacrifice, by the way. It was the LORD's good gift to Israel. But our King's praises are even more precious because they are a gospel invitation to fix our eyes on the risen King and keep trusting the God who delivered him from death.

The 'salvation' he prayed for in verse 29 means *the experience of God's righteousness*: God's goodness that flows out of him in forgiveness and love, his compassion with which he rules creation, his justice and richness that fill his people's lives with blessing. The king's experience of God's righteousness is described in detail in Psalm 71, and its words are a good approximation for the sort of praise Jesus plans to sing here in verse 30:

> Your righteousness, God, reaches to the heavens,
>   you who have done great things.
>   Who is like you, God?
> Though you have made me see troubles,
>   many and bitter,
>   you will restore my life again;
> from the depths of the earth
>   you will again bring me up.
> You will increase my honour
>   and comfort me once more.
> (Psalm 71:19–21)

God's greater purpose (69:32–36)

The cross is a singularity. On one side of it lies chaos, injustice, hatred, sorrow and evil. On the other side lies order, peace, love, joy and goodness. The destruction of the wicked has allowed the righteous one to escape their clutches and emerge into life, and as he does so, we see that he's not alone. His salvation opens a door for a great company of the poor and needy to share in God's righteousness along with him. The connection between them is underlined by a play on the word 'afflicted' in verse 29 ('*ānî* in Hebrew) and the word 'poor' in verse 32 ('*ānāv*):

> ³²The poor will see and be glad –
>> you who seek God, may your hearts live!
> ³³The LORD hears the needy
>> and does not despise his captive people.

The people who benefit from the King's resurrection are afflicted like him. They are poor in spirit, they mourn, they are meek, and they hunger and thirst for righteousness.

This is God's greater purpose in the humiliation of his king and the judgment of his enemies. The Israel that rejected its king was destroyed, but in God's wisdom Israel's destruction opened the way for a new Israel, first Jews and then Gentiles as well, to receive an inheritance in the land, in the living presence of God:

> ³⁴Let heaven and earth praise him,
>> the seas and all that move in them,
> ³⁵for God will save Zion
>> and rebuild the cities of Judah.
> Then people will settle there and possess it;
>> ³⁶the children of his servants will inherit it,
>> and those who love his name will dwell there.

We enjoy the firstfruits of that salvation today through the Spirit of Christ who dwells in us and among us; but the physicality of the psalm's final verses is important. God's purposes for us are not complete until the heavens and the earth are renewed and we live with imperishable bodies in a new creation, a creation that takes up and re-echoes the praises Christ's people will sing day and night in praise of their Redeemer.

On suffering with the Messiah

Sharing in the sufferings of Christ

The detail I find most poignant about Jesus in this psalm is in verses 13–18. The loving and compassionate Father closed his ears to the desperate cries of his child. How could God harden his heart like that? Well, it turns out he didn't. He was demonstrating his compassion for the poor, the outcast, the humble and oppressed – ensuring, as verse 6 says, that they would not be disgraced because of Jesus. As a friend of mine likes to say, it was evil that took Jesus to the cross, but it was love that held him there. And that love forges a bond between Christ and his people.

None of us are prophets as David and Jeremiah were, but we all have the prophetic word of the gospel, and speaking it inevitably attracts hostility. If you let people see Jesus in you too clearly, they'll take out their hatred of Jesus on you. The spiritual realm is watching you too, and as long as the devil roams the world your faithfulness will attract spiritual attacks – discouragement and despair, even your struggles with sin.

The fact that these hardships come to you as a result of your faithfulness makes them a sharing in the sufferings of Christ. As another friend of mine once wrote, 'Even in our most despairing, God-doubting depressions, we are permitted to say: I suffer with the Messiah. He and I are alongside each other in suffering.'[5] And that means we are permitted to say Psalm 69 as our own as well. To lament as Jesus did.

What does the victorious Christian life look like? In Paul's words, it looks like 'carry[ing] around in our body the death of Jesus, so that the life of Jesus may also be revealed in our body' (2 Corinthians 4:10).

It means being hated without reason, and complaining to God, but leaving moral superiority behind. It means being victimized, perhaps by enemies of God within the church, but caring for the welfare of the church before your own vindication. It means having unbelieving family members ashamed of you and hostile, but holding on to your Christian witness even when you know eyes will roll and tempers flare. It means rising to defend the honour of Jesus when he is dishonoured, especially by people who call themselves Christian.

Some of the most painful sufferings Christians endure come from wolves in the church, who don't have the excuse of ignorance, and who can wield Scripture expertly. Those who are God's enemies betray themselves by their scorn, by their refusal of weakness, by their willingness to humiliate, by their wilful misrepresentation and by their determination to crush the enemy by fair means or foul.

Being a victorious Christian means holding firmly to truth but weakly to power. It means humbly entrusting yourself to God in prayer and gently speaking the gospel. And it means lamenting – leaving vengeance to God and telling your pain to him instead; trusting that the world will see Christ's glory through your weakness as you stubbornly refuse to lose confidence in his love, even when he remains absent from your life.

That is a life through which God's glory will shine, a life against which the wicked will break themselves, a life in which the humble will see God and the heavens praise him.

Praying for the judgment of others

The judgment of God's enemies is a difficult subject, especially for people who are not particularly suffering at their hands. In the history of salvation, Israel – the nation that was utterly destroyed for its rejection of God – was eventually brought through death to new life beyond exile. In Psalm 69:33 there is a hint of this hope for the damned in the reference to captive people. But we need to be careful, because this is a covenantal hope but not an individual hope, and the New Testament applies it to Israel as a nation in Romans 11, but not to Judas, say, as an individual.

The starting-point for our use of the words in verses 22–28 is recognizing that this prayer only belongs to us through its fulfilment in Christ. It is a prayer against the enemies of God whose judgment Christ died to accomplish. You will never know who falls into this category until Christ has returned to judge and all secrets are brought into the open. So here is a good rule of thumb: do not use this prayer against anyone whose name you know. The Bible teaches us to pray that our enemies might repent and become God's friends. Stephen's last words as the members of the Sanhedrin stoned him to death were, 'Lord, do not hold this sin against them' (Acts 7:60).

But at the same time, we remember that the judgment of God's enemies was one of the reasons for Christ's death, and so we pray for that judgment to be accomplished. In fact we already do this every time we pray 'Your kingdom come, your will be done', because we know that at Christ's return every enemy of Jesus will be destroyed (compare 2 Thessalonians 1:5–10).

When we pray Psalm 69:22–28 in Christ, we are praying for his return to judge evil and set things right, to be sure. But we also want God to bring relief to his children by rescuing them *now* from those destined for judgment *then*. This is a prayer we should especially pray, I think, as we intercede for the persecuted church. But it is not a prayer we can direct towards any individual, no matter how evil. Even Saul who persecuted Christ's church was saved. So I'm going to finish with a prayer for the persecuted church, in the spirit of Psalm 69:

> Loving Father, we pray for your persecuted and oppressed children around the world, and we ask that you take note of those who persecute them. May the faithfulness of those they harm open their blind eyes to the love of Christ and bring them to repentance and faith in him. But for those who with open eyes seek to make a mockery of Christ's love by destroying his people and extinguishing the knowledge of God on earth, for those who knowingly make themselves your enemies for all time, we pray that you would quickly bring about their appointed judgment. Pour out your wrath on them; let your

fierce anger overtake them. And so may you finally defeat the devil and all his works, and cleanse the world of the evil that brought your Son to the cross. For we ask it in the name of Jesus Christ our Lord. Amen.

4

Psalm 88:
despair and endurance

Living with the absence of God

Being God's people means being saved, treasured, filled with new life and hope. But it does not mean being sheltered from times of trial, from terrible crises, from deep sadness, from hurt and trauma and the shadow of death. In these times the Psalms show us how to voice our troubles, how to lament. As we saw with Psalm 69, these words include telling our present troubles to God, remembering who he is and having the courage to trust him for a better day. This is the pattern of lament that the Psalms gives us, in wonderful variety, over and over again. But not always. In this study we reach the nadir of the book of Psalms, the lowest depths of its story arc. In Book III of the Psalms we see the nation die as God makes himself its enemy. The psalms that bracket Book III place question marks over the main themes of the book of Psalms. When God becomes the enemy, the wisdom of Psalm 1 stops working (Psalm 73). The hope of Psalm 2 dries up (Psalm 89).

And here at the low point we find words for the person who cannot find the strength to hope. God knows that even though hope defines Christ's people, we are still vulnerable to despair. And so in his wisdom he has given us two psalms – Psalms 88 and 89 – to help us endure. Not to overcome, but, like Job, to endure.

I will say something about Psalm 89 at the end, but for most of this study we will be in Psalm 88: three terrible cries from an individual into whose life no single ray of light shines. The psalm is described as a *maskil* of Heman the Ezrahite. Both his name and the term *maskil* have associations with wisdom and insight. Even despair is something we can express wisely or foolishly.

Few lines of modern poetry are more famous than Dylan Thomas's rejection of hope in the face of death:

Do not go gentle into that good night,
Old age should burn and rave at close of day;
Rage, rage against the dying of the light.[1]

There's a wild wisdom in the way those words respond to the absence of God. But it is not God's wisdom. Psalm 88 is far more radical. Its enemy is not death, because the enemy in Psalm 88 – the only enemy – is God. And more radical still, from beginning to end the psalmist addresses himself directly to God. There is a terrible contradiction between the God he believes in and the God he experiences, and by speaking directly to the God he believes in he refuses to let go of that contradiction.

Many Christians in times of great distress find it difficult, even impossible, to pray. So God has given us words for when we can't pray. Words to help us endure. Let's have a look at them.

The competing realities of Psalm 88

Psalm 88 is composed as three cries: the first in verse 1, the second in the middle of verse 9 and the third in verse 13 (see Figure 4). (For those of you who wonder about the word *Selah*, placed into the margin by the NIV, it's used in this psalm to mark a shift in emphasis within a stanza, not a division between stanzas.) In each cry the speaker stands before the throne of God and calls him by name, 'LORD'. And each cry is placed in a timeframe: 'day and night' (v. 1); 'every day' (v. 9); 'in the morning' (v. 13).

1–2	FIRST CRY	9b	SECOND CRY	13	THIRD CRY
3	self-description	10	'the dead'	14	self-description
6	accusation			16	accusation
8	friends, darkness	12	darkness	18	friends, darkness

Figure 4 **Clues to the structure of Psalm 88**

It's as if the act of crying out to God places the psalmist in the world of daylight, where time flows normally, and he's in front of God where his prayers are easily heard. But the prayers themselves inhabit another reality, and each one ends in darkness. Verse 9: 'my eyes are dim'; verse 12: 'place of darkness'; verse 18: 'darkness is my closest friend'. In Hebrew the first word of the psalm is 'LORD', and the last word is 'darkness'.

The central cry stands out from the others because it speaks not of the psalmist himself but of the dead in general. But let's begin with the first cry.

First cry (88:1–9a)

The God who saves

Verse 1 opens with a confession of faith, grounded in history, reinforced by experience, and it stands over the psalm like a challenge:

> [1]LORD, you are the God who saves me . . .

'I am someone you saved,' says the psalmist, 'and that binds you to me by the promise contained in the name "LORD". It means I have the right to be standing here before you, an expectation of help.' The thrice-repeated cry that follows that confession conveys intense urgency:

> . . . day and night I cry out to you.
> [2]May my prayer come before you;
>   turn your ear to my cry.

The dying of the light

The reason for this emotional intensity is simple: the light is draining out of the poet's life:

> [3]I am overwhelmed with troubles
>   and my life draws near to death.

Verse 3 begins with a close-up on the troubles that fill his consciousness and squeeze out everything good and life-giving. Then the next line pulls back to view that life, himself, seen as a whole, sliding down towards the underworld and death. He's reached the point where he has no resources left, his powers of recovery are exhausted, and he's sliding down a muddy slope towards the edge of a cliff, unable even to dig his fingers in. Every movement in this cry is downwards.

The camera pulls back further in verse 4 so that he's now seeing himself from the outside, as though he were someone else:

> ⁴I am counted among those who go down to the pit;
>   I am like one without strength.

He watches himself receding, and as he slides away from himself he loses his ability to do anything, to act. After drawing near to death in verse 3, he performs no other actions in these nine verses. Instead, bad things get done to him. He gets counted; he gets his strength scooped out of him, leaving an empty shell; and he gets 'set apart' in verse 5, a word that describes a person of no further use to their master, someone who's released from service into a precarious existence on the street:

> ⁵I am set apart with the dead,
>   like the slain who lie in the grave,
> whom you remember no more,
>   who are cut off from your care.

He's not just like the 'dead'; he's like the 'slain' – the prematurely, violently dead. His body, completely objectified now, lies discarded and motionless among the corpses in a mass grave.

What life-events lie behind this bleak poetry? Metastatic cancer? Domestic abuse? Displacement by war? The death of one's child? Extreme persecution for the faith? As with almost all the psalms, the inspired poet has de-identified himself enough so that his words can give voice to all these life-situations and more. Whatever the circumstances, here is a person whose slide into darkness feels permanent, night and day, day and night.

And yet. Pulling people back from the brink is one of the specialties of the LORD who saves. The Psalms are full of testimonies to dramatic rescues. All that's needed is for God to hear his prayer and remember him.

But if God decided to forget, then there would truly be no hope left. By the end of verse 5 the psalmist is not quite despairing, but he's close. The 'care' of God, the hand of God, is what reaches down and pulls a person out of the pit. But there's a dark door at the bottom of the pit which leads to the grave, and through that door God's hand does not reach. The poet is not dead yet, but it's getting hard to tell, and God chooses to forget the dead. He severs their connection to him.

According to Psalm 8, being remembered by God is what makes us human in the first place. Death is not a place where the angels preserve you to gaze lovingly down on your grieving family. It is not an afterlife where you get to tell jokes with Uncle Stan again. It is a terrible, dark pit, in which everything that connects you to life is systematically removed. Whatever it is that makes you *you* is destroyed, and your Creator and Sustainer turns away, shuts the door, and leaves what used to be a person diminished and decaying in the dark.

The God who destroys

And so finally the psalmist slides from despondency into despair. He's seen the trajectory of his life and drawn the logical conclusion. The God who is able to save those he loves is not saving *him*. God is the one responsible:

> 6You have put me in the lowest pit,
>   in the darkest depths.
> 7Your wrath lies heavily on me;
>   you have overwhelmed me with all your waves.

Verse 6 is a cascade of superlatives: not just the pit, but the lowest, the darkest, the deepest. This is special treatment. For some inexplicable reason he is the object of God's wrath. It is not 6 feet of earth weighing down on him, but 600 fathoms of wrath, and not just weighing but crashing down like a massive surf.

Once again, what could a person be going through to make them conclude that God was intentionally crushing the life out of them? In Psalm 32, God's heavy hand was just what David needed to drive him to his knees. But there's no confession of sin here in Psalm 88, nothing to make God's 'wrath' an act of punishment. There are no human enemies to oppress him, just friends, whose only purpose for being in the psalm is to be taken away:

> [8] You have taken from me my closest friends
> and have made me repulsive to them.
> I am confined and cannot escape;
> [9] my eyes are dim with grief.

'Repulsive' in verse 8 is a word that suggests revulsion upon revulsion, the stench of death. Even Ebola sufferers are sometimes cared for by family members who refuse to leave, though it could mean death to stay. But God has ensured that this person's isolation will be absolute. That his living days will be indistinguishable from the loneliness of the grave.

God finishes the job by immobilizing him, perhaps with shame. Even if he could find some strength to stir himself and rejoin life, he *could* not. By now he has no more tears to shed. Tears take a bit of passion, a little life.

To accuse God of destroying your life is a fearful thing to do. Three things all have to be true before you dare to talk like this. You have to be convinced that God is in control, that nothing is beyond his power to change. You have to be convinced that he cares, that he listens. And you have to be convinced that what's happened to you threatens those truths. There are some things that don't just knock the life out of us; they also threaten the divinity of God. And with that at stake there are very few limits to what we dare to say. One piece of wisdom from this psalm: you should say those things to God, not about him.

Second cry (88:9b–12)

The one thing – the only thing – that still functions in the psalmist's life is his voice. And so he uses it to cry out a second time, to 'spread out his hands', meaning to pray:

I call to you, LORD, every day;
   I spread out my hands to you.

Call it an act of hope, a gesture of defiance, a small piece of resistance as he slides into oblivion. Whatever it is, it's the one remaining sign that he's not dead yet.

And once he's made the effort to speak, he finds that he has some energy to argue, even to show some aggression – which is what rhetorical questions are. A big verbal stick. And I must say that his questions in verses 10–12 seem rather desperate:

^{10}Do you show your wonders to the dead?
   Do their spirits rise up and praise you?
^{11}Is your love declared in the grave,
   your faithfulness in Destruction?
^{12}Are your wonders known in the place of darkness,
   or your righteous deeds in the land of oblivion?

It's the crude appeal of the condemned man. 'What's the benefit to *you* of letting me die?' Or perhaps less crudely, 'This is just wrong! I want to be able to rejoice in you, to sing salvation songs, to be your light to the world!'

But there is more going on than this. Because his argument is not just personal. It concerns the dead in general, and the implications of their existence for a God who is the God of the living.

The God of the living

The first pair of questions, in verse 10, opposes two extremes. At one extreme is God, whose personhood is absolute, the source of his own life and of all other life as well. At the other extreme are the spirits of the dead, the shadowy after-images of living persons, possessing whatever diminished remnants of personhood might have survived to inhabit the underworld. They are shadows precisely because they exist beyond the light of God's personhood. If they didn't, they wouldn't be dead! They would rise up and praise him. But they don't because there is an impenetrable barrier between God and the dead.

The questions in verses 11 and 12 focus not on people but on *places* – the grave, Destruction, darkness, oblivion – and then *activities* utterly opposed to those places.

'Love' and 'faithfulness' is a pair of words the Psalms use to describe God's unshakeable commitment to David and Israel. His love and faithfulness fill all of creation and time. They are witnessed by all peoples to the ends of the earth. But not in the grave.

'Wonders' and 'righteous deeds' are the amazing things God does for people that lead them to praise him. Being rescued from the brink of death is a classic example (as in Psalm 40:9–10). Each person who experiences God's wonders contributes their testimony to the community, and deepens everyone's knowledge of the God who saves. Each praising voice strengthens the community's witness to the world and to the next generation. But not to the dead.

Did you notice the escalation of words for death? First 'the grave', then 'Destruction', meaning the place of violent death, then 'darkness', from which God's presence is withdrawn, and finally 'oblivion', from which God's remembrance is withdrawn. There's no mistaking a wave of divine wrath rising through these terms.

Whenever God subjects one of his own to untimely death – for whatever reason – the assembly of the righteous loses one member. The witness of God's people to the world gets a bit weaker, the faith of the next generation a touch less secure.

Death is a huge challenge to God's goodness and wisdom – to his being – because it's a sphere in which God is not present as God. God is God of the living. Only the living. So it makes no sense that he would diminish the sphere of his sovereignty by adding to the dead.

Second, notice how selective is the list of things that the dead don't do. This is not because the dead do other things, such as building houses or lamenting or cursing God. It's because the things the poet names are the opposites of death. They are what it means to be alive.

This is deeply significant. To praise God is to be alive. To be alive is to praise God. It's such a profound truth that the psalms even claim it for non-living things:

> Let the heavens rejoice, let the earth be glad;
>   let the sea resound, and all that is in it.
> Let the fields be jubilant, and everything in them;
>   let all the trees of the forest sing for joy.
> Let all creation rejoice before the LORD . . .
> (Psalm 96:11–13a)

Creation praises God just by existing. Humans are the most precious things in creation because their sign of life is to praise God in words for his love and righteous deeds.

So when God adds to the number of the dead, he does not just diminish the sphere of his sovereignty; he diminishes the reflection of his own glory in creation. When he thrusts one of his people into the darkness, the rest of the world gets a bit darker also. This, too, makes no sense.

If death is a place, it is not to be found within the heavens, the earth, the sea or all creation, because it's the place where there is no praise. The place of non-life. But death can reach into this world from its nowhere, and the most basic sign of its creeping presence is not sickness or pain or anguish, but the absence of praise. We know that the poor poet of Psalm 88 is on the verge of death because there is no praise left in his body.

Third cry (88:13–18)

The God who hides his face
In a normal lament this is the point where we would remember God's acts of salvation, take the courage to trust that God will be that God to us, and imagine praising him when he rescues us. But

not in this psalm. Its third cry comes in the morning, a time of hope;
but in the east no sun has risen:

> ¹³But I cry to you for help, LORD;
>   in the morning my prayer comes before you.
> ¹⁴Why, LORD, do you reject me
>   and hide your face from me?

The poet uses a Hebrew word in verse 13, meaning 'cry for help', that
plays on 'saves me' back in verse 1. He hasn't abandoned his faith in
who God is. Verse 14 is the question of someone who longs to be close
to God, whose whole being still strains desperately towards him.

But God remains absent from this man's life, and he does not
know the reason why. The God of his experience doesn't line up with
the God of his faith – and as much as anything else it's the not
knowing why that makes the constant disappointment so difficult.
Disappointment can be endured for a while – for quite a long time
when levels of trust are high. But erode trust with incomprehension,
and prolong disappointment for long enough, and eventually something deep down will break:

> ¹⁵From my youth I have suffered and been close to death;
>   I have borne your terrors and am in despair.
> ¹⁶Your wrath has swept over me;
>   your terrors have destroyed me.
> ¹⁷All day long they surround me like a flood;
>   they have completely engulfed me.
> ¹⁸You have taken from me friend and neighbour –
>   darkness is my closest friend.

Verse 15 has often been taken as describing a chronically ill person,
and though of course the psalm gives a voice to people suffering
chronic pain and sickness, the language isn't restrictive. 'Close to
death' parallels the 'terrors' of death in line 2. For his whole life,
I think, the writer has been conscious of being a breath away from
death, and now that death has shown its face he's paralysed. He's
got no more strength to take the fight back to God, and in verses 16

and 17 four lines of terror flood over the poem in a series of waves that finally overcome him. Each unanswered prayer, each unanswered question, each task for which he has no more strength or joy, each friend and colleague he loses, is another cold wave dumping him beneath the surf, and he has stopped struggling. Darkness, he tells God, is all he knows.

I'm quite certain that among those reading this there is more than one of you inhabiting this psalm right now. So let me say before anything else how incredibly encouraging I find the person who wrote this poem. He was a faithful Israelite, and his experience of God was one of long disappointment and lonely sorrow. But still he clings to God as his Saviour, despite not knowing why God doesn't save him. He refuses to go gentle into the night, but neither does he rage against his Maker. As he sinks away, he clings to God. Can you think of anything more impressive?

The context of Psalm 88

As we move towards Christian reflection, I want to step back to the context for a moment. Book III of the Psalter is just seventeen psalms long. It echoes the period in salvation history when the kingdoms of Israel and Judah were slowly and irreversibly sliding towards death. Laments bracket the book at each end, and while there are some praise psalms, there's no thanksgiving. Instead, there are three psalms of warning in the middle (Psalms 78; 81; 82). The theme that unfolds is 'How long?' How long, LORD, will the enemy mock you? How long will you hide yourself? How long will your anger smoulder against the prayers of your people?

The death of the nation is easier to understand than the suffering of the poet in Psalm 88. Israel's destruction came only after repeated warnings, and it was well deserved. And yet the question 'How long?' remains, because alongside the promise to abandon his people if they abandoned him, God had made an unconditional promise to David that his line would never die out.

Psalm 89 is another *maskil* written by another Ezrahite, Ethan. Its opening verses affirm again and again that the LORD's covenant love stands for ever, and the rest of the psalm entrenches this truth, to make the breaking of the covenant with David as incomprehensible as possible. The paired words in Psalm 88:11, 'love' and 'faithfulness', are used more in Psalm 89 than anywhere else. As the psalm draws to a close it sounds more and more like Psalm 88, and, as in that psalm, its cries of desperation receive no reply:

> How long, LORD? Will you hide yourself for ever?
>   How long will your wrath burn like fire?
> Remember how fleeting is my life.
>   For what futility you have created all humanity!
> Who can live and not see death,
>   or who can escape the power of the grave?
> Lord, where is your former great love,
>   which in your faithfulness you swore to David?
> (Psalm 89:46–49)

These words give us a context or frame for viewing the individual of Psalm 88. His words of despairing faith are preserved as a *maskil* to be spoken in the congregation. What are the people supposed to learn from it? Well, they have known God's silence in their national life, and they don't understand why God has abandoned his anointed one in the face of his promise. It seems to me that Psalm 88 is there to help them interpret that experience. Here is an individual who does not deserve to suffer, but who despairs of seeing the face of the God who saves. And yet he clings on. If this is how a righteous person behaves in such dire straits, how much more should they who deserved their judgment cling on in trust.

Death, Jesus and us

Psalm 88 and the nature of death

In the larger sweep of salvation history, the mockery and death of God's anointed is an important pointer to the death of Jesus. And Psalm 88, even more than Psalm 89, opens a window for us onto

Jesus' experience. It does this in the first place by leading us to reflect on the nature of death.

Psalm 88 isn't a psalm about death. It's a psalm about the suffering caused by the nearness of death. But it has important things to say about death along the way. They are important because too often, I think, the hope of resurrection leads Christians to minimize the horrors of death. But just look at the terrible wounds death leaves behind on the living, wounds which time may never heal. Those are tokens of the horrors of death itself.

Death opens a door to a world without God, because God is a God of life. Israel's faith was unique in its understanding of death, and those of us who live and work across cultures appreciate just what a difference it makes to know the truth about death. Death is not a numinous power or a god to be appeased. It's not a portal to a dark country that is opened by a sinister spirit. It's not a source of mysterious beings who walk invisibly among us. Whatever shadowy existence the dead continue to have, it does not amount to life, any more than the dead amount to persons, or have relationships, or know God's love. Our dead ancestors do not concern themselves with us, or with anything, because they are gone. Gone from life and light and love and wonder. They are lifeless, powerless, hopeless, inert. They are crushed, destroyed, cut off, silent. There is nothing more terrible and more pitiful than death.

Now of course death is not the last word. Even God's enemies will be raised on the last day to face judgment, as Daniel 12 teaches us. And those who are united with Christ by faith receive a share, even now, in his resurrection. So we don't pass into death as those without hope. Neither do we fear death, though naturally we fear dying – not that we need to, because wonderfully we do not die alone. As we live in Christ, so we die in Christ, and at his return we will rise, as he did, to inhabit imperishable bodies. So yes, death is not the last chapter in our story.

But none of that makes death any less terrible.

Listen to this piece of advice from Nicholas Wolterstorff, written in the aftermath of the death of his son, killed in an accident at the age of twenty-five:

What do you say to someone who is suffering? . . . please: Don't say it's not really so bad. Because it is. Death is awful, demonic. If you think your task as comforter is to tell me that really, all things considered, it's not so bad, you do not sit with me in my grief but place yourself off in the distance away from me. Over there, you are of no help. What I need to hear from you is that you recognize how painful it is. I need to hear from you that you are with me in my desperation. To comfort me, you have to come close. Come sit beside me on my mourning bench.

I know: People do sometimes think things are more awful than they really are. Such people need to be corrected – gently, eventually. But no one thinks death is more awful than it is. It's those who think it's not so bad that need correcting.[2]

Psalm 88 and the death of Jesus

It's only when we refuse to sugarcoat death with easy talk of resurrection that we can start to imagine how much more unthinkable it was for the Lord Jesus to die than it is for you and me:

- When *we* die, the breath of life that God lent us is taken away because we leave his presence. But Jesus' life was native to him, a permanent gift of the Father rising up from within him like a spring of living water.
- When *we* die, our bodies return to the dust from which they were made. But when Jesus died, the one in whom all things were created was cast out of creation. The light of the world was extinguished by the darkness.

God was pleased to have all his fullness dwell in Christ. To die to all that fullness, to enter a place where God is not . . . I don't think we are capable of grasping just how fundamentally against Christ's nature it was to die; how abhorrently Death tore into the fabric of his being. Death isn't really a stranger to us mortals. From the moment we're born we start to die. But even after Jesus was born as a man, death had no power over him. He was the one who had power over death, as he showed when he made the deaf hear and gave sight to the blind, and when he called the dead back from the grave.

Jesus didn't share *our* death; he endured *his* death, alone, for us. In him God gave himself to the one domain where he was utterly foreign.

As Jesus hung dead on the cross, Luke observes in his Gospel that 'all those who knew him, including the women who had followed him from Galilee, stood at a distance, watching these things' (Luke 23:49). Luke has in mind the Greek version of Psalm 88:8, which says: 'you set those who knew me at a distance.' We're right to hear Psalm 88 on the lips of Jesus, and when we do, we hear something far more terrible than any of us will ever know.

Perhaps you are someone who has wept despairingly before God again and again, but been met by silence. The Bible has lost its power to speak, or prayer to comfort. How do you endure? I don't know. But Psalm 88 gives you one thing to cling on to. It gives you the death of Jesus, a suffering that surrounds yours, as vast as the desert sky surrounding the moon. A suffering that knows everything you've endured, and endures it with you. A suffering that assures you that God knows and understands.

Does this explain anything? I don't think so. Does it help you move on? Probably not. But sometimes our task is simply to endure.

The fact that Jesus' death does not answer all our questions is important to remember. Why does God choose to suffer in the first place? Did Jesus really have to die? If you think about it, he had the power to call people back from death without needing to die himself.

I've often heard people answer this question by saying, 'It was the only way God could have dealt with the problem of sin and evil.' But how do we know that? Where does the Bible say that? How do we know that there was not a glorious and awesome arbitrariness to God's decision to deal with sin *this* way?

What do we know *Jesus* knew about the reasons for his death? He knew what his death would achieve, and he knew how. But as he watched death open its mouth to swallow him, I'm not sure that he knew the answer to the question 'Why have you forsaken me?'

(Mark 15:34). What I do know is that he clung to God even as God broke and destroyed him.

The death of Jesus is a deep mystery. God does not finally explain suffering, either ours or his. But his choice to suffer means something profound for our own suffering. It doesn't make suffering in itself noble or godlike – though some Christian traditions have mistakenly drawn that conclusion. But it does make suffering a unique medium for displaying godlikeness. It shows us that when we suffer in faith, we live as God's image in the world.

Despairing and enduring together

The gospel is good news. It brings joy and blessing, and creates a community marked by thanks and praise. Unfortunately it can also make us a community in which broken and grieving people stand unnoticed outside the circle of the light. I want to offer just two suggestions.

First. Not many of us share the experience of this psalm, but you may find yourself sitting alongside a brother or sister who does. When you do, you should remember the honesty of this poet. He is way beyond pious euphemisms, and the accusations he levels against God may be shocking, but they betray a deep conviction that God is in control, that the only arms into which he can run for safety are the arms that have thrust him into darkness. That's hard. And we ought to respect and admire that painful honesty. We need to not be like Job's friends and make a cage out of our piety. We need to remember, as Wolterstorff puts it, 'Instead of explaining our suffering God shares it.'[3] So let's not try to explain suffering, but be content simply to share it, as God does.

Second. I was deeply encouraged recently by a conversation with a former student, Scott. He spoke about the experience of hearing Psalm 88 read in church two days after the sudden death of his wife Susie. He said that he felt this psalm understood him better than anything else. It gave him permission to be devastated. And this made me think of all the other Scotts in the many churches we all attend. Of what a grave disservice we do them by never lamenting together.

When someone sings a lament from the front, or when we say a psalm of lament together, we are not just giving grieving people permission to grieve. We are entering into an experience of grieving together which can be meaningful for each of us. Lament strips back our shiny veneer to lay bare the darkness that lies within, and which most of us, most of the time, successfully conceal. And lament strengthens us to endure – even when darkness presses in with no sign of relief – because the God we cry to is the Lord who has walked this dark road ahead of us, and who now shines a word of promise back along the path to direct our feet to safety.

The book of Psalms is filled with laments. God has given them to us to sing or otherwise perform together. For most of us, this will be a countercultural exercise. Modern society shrinks in horror from acute sorrow and grief. It's challenging and uncomfortable. But perhaps that's a sign of how much we in the church need to recover lament.[4]

5

Psalm 91:
the LORD is with you

Book IV of the Psalms: after the fall

We have moved just three psalms forwards from our last study, but we've reached a turning-point. By Psalm 89 the nation is lying in ruins, the kingship has failed and the Davidic covenant is torn up. The vision from Psalm 2 of the LORD and his anointed ruling the nations has evaporated. Logically, Book IV should reflect the darkness of exile. And sure enough, this short collection of just seventeen psalms ends with a prayer for God to gather the people of Israel from the nations and bring them back to the land.

And yet Book IV serves up two big surprises. First, instead of beginning with a psalm of Babylonian exile, it goes in the opposite direction and opens with the oldest of all the psalms – a prayer of Moses that begins:

> LORD, you have been our dwelling-place
>   throughout all generations.
> (Psalm 90:1)

And the Book ends the same way, with a great trilogy of psalms (104 – 106) that retell the history of the world from creation to the exodus, ending with Israel's rebellion in the days of Moses and the judges. The theme of the trilogy is God's faithfulness in the face of Israel's sinfulness. This is such an unexpected way to respond to the failure of the kingdom – and it's brilliant! Book IV is making the point that the exile was not the first time Israel went kingless. In the days when God was Israel's only king, he judged his people by the law of Moses, and he forgave them because of his promise to Abraham. Maybe God could still rule an exiled people, even without an anointed king.

That's surprise number one. The second surprise is delivered by Psalms 91 – 100. With Psalms 88 and 89 still bitter in our mouths, we suddenly find ourselves in the longest stretch of pure praise in all the Psalms. It celebrates God as our Rock and Fortress, the God of all the earth before whom distant shores rejoice and the nations tremble – including every nation where Israel has been scattered. The LORD is the great Saviour who stirs his people to sing a new song and be glad. And once the kick of adrenalin settles a bit and we start to pay some attention, we notice something very unusual about these psalms. The king is not mentioned in any of them – not once! You can find Zion, the temple, priests, Jacob and Judah. But not the king. Instead, we hear the line 'The LORD reigns!' again and again: in Psalms 93, 96, 97, 99. It could also be translated 'The LORD has become king!' It's a sentence never used outside these psalms. (Some scholars discern a king in Psalm 91, but I think the psalm points in another direction, as we shall see.)

In short, Psalm 91 is the first in a group of psalms that responds to the failure of human kingship by celebrating the direct, unmediated, kingship of God. None of these psalms even names its human author. It's as if they had descended from heaven like giant loudspeakers booming God's praises across the earth.

Introducing Psalm 91

Its boldness

An American friend of mine was in an airport terminal some years ago, where she overheard a woman on the phone with someone who had evidently suffered some kind of tragedy. At one point the woman said, 'Honey, you need to dial Psalm 911!' It took my friend a moment, but she figured it out: Psalm 91 verse 1.

Psalm 91 has always been an 'emergency' psalm for people in trouble – and so it should be. But not everyone goes to this psalm for the right reasons. As early as the first century AD, people were wearing amulets to protect against demons with 'You will not fear the pestilence that stalks in the darkness' written inside them. Or maybe you've been in a house with a plaque on the wall that says, 'He will command his angels concerning you to guard you in all your ways.' Some Christians wrote that on their walls in the days of the early church. I've been told there are buses in Namibia that have signs saying, 'Protected by Psalm 91'.

As we study this psalm I hope we will learn to fully embrace it as our '911' psalm, in all its unqualified positivity, but without sliding into unreality or superstition.

Its structure

Psalm 91 is divided into three parts by changes of speaker (see Figure 5). In the first part a faithful Israelite claims, 'The LORD is my refuge.' Then in verse 3 we hear a new voice, a priest or a prophet, answering the faithful Israelite with words of reassurance: 'Surely he will save you.' This second part divides in two at verse 9, where the faithful Israelite's confession is quoted. In the third part we hear the LORD himself speaking, giving the faithful Israelite his personal assurance of protection.

	Speaker	Speech	
Part 1	A faithful Israelite:	'The LORD is my refuge'	91:1–2
Part 2a	A priest or prophet:	'Surely the LORD will save you'	91:3–8
Part 2b		'No harm will overtake you'	91:9–13
Part 3	The LORD:	'Because he loves me'	91:14–16

Figure 5 **Clues to the structure of Psalm 91**

The faithful Israelite

A bold claim (91:1–2)

The opening verses make a bold claim:

> [1]Whoever dwells in the shelter of the Most High
>   will rest in the shadow of the Almighty.

²I will say of the LORD, 'He is my refuge and my fortress,
  my God, in whom I trust.'

Two images here shape the rest of the psalm. The first is the image of a traveller who 'dwells' and 'rests'. Imagine you are alone in a foreign city and your bag has been stolen with passport, money, ID, phone, everything. It's not a safe city, and you're sitting on a dusty step figuring out whether to try the local police, who will need a hefty bribe, when a married couple and their two kids walk past. They ask if you're OK, they hear your story and they say, 'Come stay with us tonight and we'll sort you out in the morning.' That's the experience of the traveller in verse 1, invited to share someone's home and hospitality, to sleep safe under their roof. But of course the benefactor here in verse 1 isn't a married couple; it's 'the Almighty' – Abraham's name for God. This is the Ancient of Days, Lord of creation and history, who sees you sitting on the dusty step and says, 'Come stay at my place.'

The second image: in verse 2 the image of shade hardens into high walls and we know there are enemies close by. God's nearness and kindness has turned into strength, and the psalmist has risen from his rest to declare himself as one who trusts in God and God alone. The key thing that his declaration does is to take those images of shelter and stronghold, and apply them to God himself. These aren't words you hang on the wall of your home to turn it into a castle. They are words that surround you with a fortress wherever you go.

Imagine you have left your dusty step and slept safe under the stranger's roof. You're at breakfast the next morning, and there's a knock at the door. A soldier strides in, stops in front of your host and snaps off a salute. 'You car's ready, General.' You do a double-take, and he looks a bit amused. But he says to you, 'I've finished my leave and it's back to headquarters. This place won't be safe when I'm gone. If you'd like to ride with us to the capital city, I'll drop you off at the embassy.' That's a travel story you'd tell more than once! But you see the point. The safest place you can be is wherever that man is. And in the case of God, that means anywhere. Having God as your refuge makes you a protected person.

The rest of the psalm fleshes out this claim by exploring various aspects of the Lord's protection. I find it a helpful approximation to think of verse 1 being fleshed out in verses 3–8, and verse 2 being fleshed out in verses 9–13. At the risk of overworking my analogy, you could call verses 3–8 'In the general's house', and verses 9–13 'In the general's motorcade'.

Words of assurance, part 1

The Lord will protect you (91:3–8)

Before we consider the argument of any psalm, it's worth simply immersing ourselves in its images, and trying to feel the emotional journey they take us on. Notice as we move through verses 3–7 how the images of God change, and how the images of danger change as well:

> ³Surely he will save you
> from the fowler's snare
> and from the deadly pestilence.
> ⁴He will cover you with his feathers,
> and under his wings you will find refuge;
> his faithfulness will be your shield and rampart.
> ⁵You will not fear the terror of night,
> nor the arrow that flies by day,
> ⁶nor the pestilence that stalks in the darkness,
> nor the plague that destroys at midday.
> ⁷A thousand may fall at your side,
> ten thousand at your right hand,
> but it will not come near you.

You start out as a small bird, and the God who rescues you is like an eagle protecting you with his body, cherishing you and holding you close. But the dangers grow, and out of his determination to keep you safe he becomes more: a wall and a body-shield so strong that you can look out from its safety at the terrors of death without a flicker of fear. The dangers grow and grow, from the terror of night when you can't see the enemy, to the madness of battle where you can't see an arrow till it hits you. And then from human enemies we escalate to the invisible, even demonic forces of verse 6. The casualties rise to apocalyptic proportions in verse 7: the whole world goes mad, but you are left impossibly standing, unscathed in a landscape of total destruction. You see what I mean about an emotional journey! But the twist comes in verse 8:

> [8]You will only observe with your eyes
>   and see the punishment of the wicked.

It turns out that all those enemies that launched themselves at your throat were God's instruments of judgment. You remain miraculously standing because God was sheltering you from a death you deserved just as much as the ten thousand around you. The only reason you didn't die was because you put your trust in God and made him your refuge.

He will protect you through a pandemic? Really?

When I was selecting a psalm from Book IV for this series of studies, the obvious place to look was in Psalms 96 – 100, with their focus on the LORD's reign over the nations, and the missionary imperative that flows from this. However, I was drawn to Psalm 91 by verse 6. The rare word 'plague' in the second line could be translated 'pandemic'. The summer school at which the talks that became this book were given was in its second year of disruption by pandemic, and if you were listening online, or if you are reading this book now, then God protected you. You survived a disease that had an official death toll of around 6 million by July 2022, but which best estimates put at roughly 22 million and counting.[1] And yet those millions of dead include many, many people whose trust in God was no less firm or well grounded than mine or yours. What does this psalm have to say about them?

I want to answer that question in three steps: by considering the Old Testament context; then Jesus; and then us, his people.

Psalm 91 and Deuteronomy 32

In the first study, I mentioned that psalms are meditations on the law. One of my goals in this study is to demonstrate that in some detail. The present psalm – a sequel to the Prayer of Moses (Psalm 90) – meditates on the Song of Moses in Deuteronomy 32, which is a prophecy of Israel's future. It begins by reminding its audience of the way God had cherished Israel in the wilderness:

> In a desert land he found him,
>   in a barren and howling waste.
> He shielded him and cared for him;
>   he guarded him as the apple of his eye,
> like an eagle that stirs up its nest
>   and hovers over its young,
> that spreads its wings to catch them
>   and carries them on its pinions.
> (Deuteronomy 32:10–11)

But then the song gets dark. It predicts that Israel will abandon the LORD for idols, and suffer all kinds of judgment:

> You deserted the Rock, who fathered you;
>   you forgot the God who gave you birth . . .
>
> '[Therefore] I will heap calamities on them
>   and spend my arrows against them.
> I will send wasting famine against them,
>   consuming pestilence and deadly plague;
> I will send against them the fangs of wild beasts,
>   the venom of vipers that glide in the dust.'
> (Deuteronomy 32:18, 23–24)

I want you to notice two things. First of all, how similar these images and words are to the ones in Psalm 91. And second, that the verses in

Deuteronomy about heaping calamity on Israel have been flipped in Psalm 91. Now the faithful person will be *protected* from calamity.

How do we interpret this? We don't know when the psalm was written; it may originally have expressed the hope of an Israelite in pre-exilic times. But by placing it here at the start of Book IV the author of the Psalms encourages us to read it against the backdrop of exile. In that context, what Psalm 91 offers a faithful Israelite is no ordinary promise of protection. It's promising them – promising Israel, actually – a do-over of their national history. The LORD is saying, 'Just as I hovered over you in the wilderness like a mother eagle, so I will hover over you again. But this time I'll protect you from the arrows and the plague that you so richly deserved before, because this time you're different. Exile has made you into a people who trust in the LORD. And because you've made him your refuge, you can look forward to a second exodus.'

Psalm 91, Jesus and us

That's the Old Testament context. None of us is an ancient Israelite, and not many of us are Jewish, but the history of Israel has become the history of all Christians through the history of the Lord Jesus. Jesus was shown to be the faithful Israelite of this wilderness psalm by his refusal of Satan's temptations during his forty days in the wilderness (Luke 4:1–13); and his faithfulness was finally vindicated by his rescue from death and his ascension to God's right hand – what Luke 9:31 calls his 'exodus' (see NIV margin).

God's promise of protection then extends from Jesus to cover each person he died for. This doesn't mean that God will spare every Christian from dying of Covid-19. But it does mean that he will protect them from *punishment* by Covid, or by any other trouble, for that matter (v. 8). We may for a time share in the sufferings of Christ, but there will not be one moment during those times when we are not sheltered beneath God's wings. There will not be one moment during which God stops being our fortress, or relaxes his determination to bring us safely to his side.

The New Testament equivalent of these verses is the famous ending of Romans 8: 'I am convinced that nothing in all creation will be able to separate us from the love of God that is in Christ Jesus our Lord.'

Words of assurance, part 2

The world cannot touch you (91:9–13)

If that was where the psalm stopped we might get away with a purely spiritual reading, in which God protects Christ and his people through danger and ultimately death in order to bring us safely to the far country where Christ awaits.

But there's more to the story. Verses 3–8 describe how God's presence protects his people – like staying in the general's house. But verses 9–13 are like riding out in the general's motorcade. We're protected by God so that we can venture out in his strength and be used by him:

> ⁹If you say, 'The LORD is my refuge,'
>   and you make the Most High your dwelling,
> ¹⁰no harm will overtake you,
>   no disaster will come near your tent.

In verse 9 the speaker, probably a priest or a prophet, reminds the faithful Israelite of his confession back in verse 2. (It's a difficult verse to translate, but its meaning is clear enough, and the NIV captures it well.) 'You've made the LORD your place of refuge? Well, this is what happens next. As you travel you're going to find yourself surrounded by evil and violence, but none of it can touch you because you're protected.' How can that promise be true? It doesn't seem realistic, does it? But let's keep reading! Verse 10 is basically a summary of verses 3–8; and it's just the beginning:

> ¹¹For he will command his angels concerning you
>   to guard you in all your ways;
> ¹²they will lift you up in their hands,
>   so that you will not strike your foot against a stone.

¹³ You will tread on the lion and the cobra;
> you will trample the great lion and the serpent.

I love the imagery of verses 11–13. In verse 11 we've got angels – supernatural helpers – who preserve us in our 'ways', meaning our *walking*. In verse 13 we do some walking, over a bunch of dangerous creatures. The last of them, the serpent, probably represents supernatural foes, to balance out the angels at the start. Then in the middle of this, verse 12, we find a lovely poetic device that the Psalms use a few times: two body parts, *hands* and *feet*, but each part belongs to a different body. It's like Psalm 8, where God made us rulers over the works of *his hands* and put everything under *our feet*. Or Psalm 110, where God says to the Messiah, 'Sit at *my right hand* until I make your enemies a footstool for *your feet*.' It's a way of describing God and his human servant acting as one.

The point is clear. God protects his people for a purpose: so that they can work together with him in the conquering of his enemies. The world can do nothing to stop us! Are you enthused? I don't want to spoil the moment, but we still need to figure out exactly what these verses are promising us, because we know the Christian life is filled with troubles. Don't forget some of the problematic applications of this psalm that we thought about at the beginning.

How far can we take these promises?

Deuteronomy 32 revisited

To help us interpret these verses, I want to repeat the procedure we used for verses 3–8, starting with Deuteronomy 32.

Israel's judgment is only the halfway point of the Song of Moses, because the exile created a new problem:

> I said I would scatter them
>   and erase their name from human memory,
> but I dreaded the taunt of the enemy,
>   lest the adversary misunderstand

and say, 'Our hand has triumphed;
  the LORD has not done all this.'
(Deuteronomy 32:26–27)

Babylon was God's instrument of judgment, but to the rest of the world it looked as though the Babylonians did it by themselves, and that their demonic gods had destroyed the God of Israel. The only way the world would see the truth about Israel's God was if Babylon was destroyed and the LORD brought his people back through the desert to the land again.

In the second half of Psalm 91 there are numerous details that point to a wilderness journey. The unusual word 'dwelling' (v. 9) is picked up from the opening of Psalm 90 to remind us that this is the sequel to the psalm of Moses. 'Tent' (v. 10) is often a poetic word for a house, but in this context it suggests an actual tent in the wilderness. The paths or 'ways' in verse 11 are clearly rough and stony and surrounded by beasts of the wild places. And then there are the the angels. Angels feature a bit in Genesis, but it's their role in the exodus story that verse 11 reflects: 'See, I am sending an angel ahead of you to guard you along the way and to bring you to the place I have prepared. Pay attention to him . . . since my Name is in him' (Exodus 23:20–21).

So the triumphant journey in Psalm 91:10–13 is a second wilderness journey, a second exodus. And if we assume that Psalm 91 is mindful of the entire Song of Moses, we can infer that the *purpose* of the journey is the vindication of God through the return of his people. Here is a final extract from Deuteronomy 32:

He will say: 'Now where are their gods,
  the rock they took refuge in . . .

'See now that I myself am he!
  There is no god besides me.
I put to death and I bring to life,
  I have wounded and I will heal,
  and no one can deliver out of my hand.'
(Deuteronomy 32:37, 39)

The reason this is significant is that it points to a work of God that is *visible to the world*. We can't just reduce the promise of Psalm 91 to spiritual blessings.

When we make the LORD our refuge we are not just shielded from his enemies; we also get to contribute to the vindication of his name. We get to be his agents in the world, not just passing safely through the dangers that lie between us and our heavenly destination, but overcoming and destroying them with his strength. 'Trample' (v. 13) doesn't mean 'step on'; it means 'crush and destroy'.

Some thoughts about angels

But what does being God's agent actually mean? Let's think about angels for a bit. Outside our secular Western culture, angels play a huge part in people's thinking, especially people from cultures in the Middle East, North Africa and parts of Asia, and from many Christian cultures too.

Our guide to interpreting verses 11 and 12 is, of all people, the devil. When he tempted Jesus to prove he was the Son of God by throwing himself from the temple, the devil quoted these verses – but he left out the second half of verse 11, 'to guard you in all your ways'. Jesus' response was another quote: 'Do not put the Lord your God to the test' (Matthew 4:7). In other words, angels don't protect us from the consequences of doing stupid things, or pursuing our own agenda. Angels are there because of the bit the devil cunningly omitted: to protect us 'in all our ways', which in the context of Psalm 91 means our walking along the path of obedience. They serve God by preserving us as agents of his kingdom. Their hands; our feet.

What sort of victories do we enjoy in partnership with angels? Lions and serpents are clearly metaphorical, and from earliest times Christian readers took cues from the way these animals feature in Scripture to suggest that they represent two types of devilish attack: concealed deception, like that of the serpent in the garden of Eden, and open attack, such as the persecutions Peter's readers faced when he called the devil a 'roaring lion' (1 Peter 5:8). Augustine, who knew a thing or two about persecution, decided that the devil is more dangerous when he flatters.[2] And he was right, of course. It's much,

much rarer for a Christian to stumble because of persecution than it is for us to stumble because of doubt or guilt or pride or selfishness.

Spiritual conflict involves material reality. In Israel's history these creatures clearly symbolized physical enemies, and salvation was physical, as it is for us too, of course, with a new creation on the way. Angels – a host of them – are there to lift you over *any* obstacle to your obedience, internal or external.

Here's the point: if we were not surrounded by angels we would all of us be squished bugs on Satan's windscreen. The perseverance of God's people is testimony to the supernatural powers that sustain each one of us from day to day. The simple fact that you wake up and say your prayers and give thanks to God for Jesus and put your hope in him for another day is a miracle. It's a public vindication of God, a public testimony to his power and presence, a public victory over every power that stands against him.

The LORD speaks

What it means to make the LORD your refuge (91:14–16)

The scenario in verse 14 is that everyone falls silent, and the LORD himself speaks. We can't be sure who he's speaking to, but I suspect it's his enemies from the previous verse. He points to the faithful Israelite and tells them, 'This one's protected.'

> ¹⁴'Because he loves me,' says the LORD, 'I will rescue him;
> I will protect him, for he acknowledges my name.'

What sort of person does the LORD make these promises to? As this psalm has already told us, it's the person who makes the LORD their refuge. But what is involved in making the LORD your refuge?

You love God

The first characteristic of the protected person is that they *love God*. The word used here for 'love' is an uncommon one. It describes strong affection that draws two people together. It means attaching yourself to Jesus your Saviour by keeping him in the forefront of your imagination, through your prayers and meditations on Scripture, your conversations, your reading and listening. It means orienting your plans and hopes around him, taking joy in his love for you, not letting other things draw your heart away from him. As Hebrews says:

> Keep your lives free from the love of money and be content with what you have, because God has said,
>
> 'Never will I leave you;
> never will I forsake you.'
> (Hebrews 13:5)

This does not mean that only people with a sufficiently intense love for Jesus will be kept safe from judgment. Our love is not a work that saves us. Anyone who confesses their need of Christ and submits to his lordship is a protected person, and there are no degrees of protection. You are kept safe from judgment or you are not.

But I think verse 14 may mean that the person whose instinct in trouble is to turn to God for help is a person more likely to be rescued from that trouble than the person who does not turn to him. The person who is attached to God is always mindful of him, and therefore they are always prayerful, and God listens to those prayers.

You know God

The second characteristic of the protected person is that they *acknowledge God's name*. That doesn't mean telling people about God, at least not in this verse. It's broader. It means knowing God's character intimately, and acting on that knowledge.

God's character, or his 'name', emerges out of the seven actions he performs in these final verses:

> ¹⁴'Because he loves me,' says the LORD, 'I will *rescue* him;
> I will *protect* him, for he acknowledges my name.

¹⁵He will call on me, and I will *answer* him;
  I will be with him in trouble,
  I will *deliver* him and *honour* him.
¹⁶With long life I will *satisfy* him
  and *show* him my salvation.'

The protected person knows God as the God who rescues, the God who protects. And how do you get to know God as those things? Easy. You do things that require him to rescue you and protect you! The central statement about God in these verses is the one in the middle of verse 15: 'I will be with him in trouble'. How do you come to know God as the God who is with you in trouble? You get into trouble!

That doesn't mean doing stupid things such as deciding you'll break an unjust law because you have freedom in Christ, and God's going to keep you out of jail; or deciding not to work for a living because God will provide. Remember the bit the devil left out of verse 11. It means boldly walking in his ways, undeterred by the consequences. The recipe for trouble verse 15 has in mind is serving Christ. And Psalm 91 promises that people who step out boldly in the service of Christ will find themselves held safe.

There is a repeated movement in these final verses: out and up. In verse 14 God draws us *out* of danger ('rescue') and lifts us *up* away from it ('protect'). In verse 15 God pulls us *out* of tight places ('deliver'), and lifts us *up* ('honour') to vindicate us in the eyes of others. This is the immediate and visible protection the psalm promises us. Whenever *obedience* leads to *trouble* leads to *rescue*, two things happen. Your experiential knowledge of God deepens, and your life becomes a clearer public witness to God's power and justice.

God gives you a satisfying life

The final verse assures us that the protected person will be *satisfied with their life*. It's a claim, like the rest of the psalm, that works out on two levels. Equating long life with God's 'salvation' suggests eternal life, and reinforces the spiritual protection that the psalm guarantees absolutely to every person who trusts in God. But 'satisfying' someone with long life is a unique expression. It points, I think, to quality of life. It reminds me of the climactic statement in Deuteronomy 30:20, 'The Lord is your life.' Think of the image of resting in the Lord. It's about *contentment*, because your life is no longer about wanting things you don't have. Now think about the image of the path across the desert. It's about *purpose* and not having to find a meaning for life and strive to fulfil it.

I remember, in a summer school back in 1984, being gripped by Elisabeth Elliot's evening talks throughout the week. She had been a missionary in Ecuador with her husband, Jim, who went with four other men to try to make contact with members of an unreached tribe, only to be killed by them. Elisabeth wrote a book about her husband's twenty-eight years of life and his violent death, and she boldly called it *Shadow of the Almighty*. You couldn't say that no harm came to Jim Elliot. But his life was a complete life, a life of integrity and love and passion and purpose. Did his bold obedience publicly vindicate God? It was an obedience that not only brought God honour but also had an impact on thousands of people, including me. Jim Elliot died a death that gave his motto its power, a motto I learned in 1984 and still know today: 'He is no fool who gives what he cannot keep to gain what he cannot lose.' But most of all – and this was Elisabeth's point, I think – Jim's life was a protected life because it was lived in the shadow of the Almighty, and his death never broke God's grip on him for a moment. Today his life has hardly even begun.

So as we seek to live this psalm, let me leave you with three suggestions.

Being confident in Christ's service

Nurture your confidence

Psalm 91 is not a talisman or charm. It does not guarantee that nothing bad will happen to you, even if you do walk faithfully in the Lord's path. You only have to think of Jesus as the fulfiller of this psalm to see that the long life it promises will not all be lived on this earth. But none of that should lessen the confidence this psalm gives us in the shelter of the Most High – confidence, especially, in the midst of trouble.

Consider the following. First, your troubles and sufferings are not punishment for your sins. They may be troubles God gives you to make you more like Jesus. Jerome once said, 'The master does not correct his disciple unless he sees signs of promise in them. But once a doctor gives up caring for their patient, it is a sign that they despair.'³ Like Job, you may never know the reason for your troubles. And actually the reason doesn't matter. The point is that you are not suffering because God is judging you.

Second, God will make sure that you are not overwhelmed by your troubles, that you conquer them. Conquering them means not being dragged away from God by them, not falling from faith. It means going through trouble the way Jesus did, prayerfully and obediently. That's treading on the lion and the cobra!

Third, God puts himself between you and trouble. He shelters you under his wings. Ultimately he will ensure that you are satisfied with long life, and that you see his salvation.

Act out your confidence

My next suggestion is to be inspired by this psalm to act out your confidence. God is your fortress. So live the life of a protected person! Remember that God protects you to be his partner in the conquering of his enemies. He surrounds you with angels. He rescues those who love him. Every time *obedience* leads to *trouble* leads to *rescue*, your knowledge of God deepens, and your confidence in the real possibility of physical protection grows. The classic example is Daniel's friends. Remember their words:

> If we are thrown into the blazing furnace, the God we serve is able to deliver us from it, and he will deliver us from Your Majesty's hand. But even if he does not, we want you to know, Your Majesty, that we will not serve your gods or worship the image of gold you have set up.
> (Daniel 3:17–18)

I love their chutzpah! And the thing is, they weren't being rash, they weren't denying reality. They simply lived life boldly as protected people. They perfectly express the nuance of Psalm 91's confidence. Like them, each of us can boldly stand up to those who oppose our faithful obedience and tell them, 'As a protected servant I know my Master can and will preserve me, body and soul. Of course, this may be my last job. I might not feel my work is finished, but God knows when it's time, and if now is the time for me to see my reward, to know at last the satisfaction of life which in this world I can only imagine, then Hallelujah! Otherwise, though, you can't touch me!'

The alternative is that we look away from God, we forget what he's done for us, we lose confidence in his promise and then we start to fear. We start to hesitate and take precautions that lead to sins such as greed or diluting the gospel. The promise of this psalm is that your decision to take shelter in God and start living as a protected person will bring you experiences of God's protection in your life that deepen your knowledge of him and make your witness to his victory all the more powerful.

Take up the challenge of mission

Finally, I want to repeat the invitation I gave at our summer school: to seriously consider the adventure of long-term, cross-cultural mission. Life is already an adventure, of course, and best of all it's an adventure in the company of the Most High God, who will ensure that the adventure ends well. So all I'm putting before you now is this: go for broke! God is inviting you to join him in trampling down Satan and bringing a people from every nation out of judgment and into his salvation.

All of us are tasked with the mission of carrying the name of God across danger, of showing the world who God is by our trust. So why not carry the name of God into more hostile or unexplored territory? You may have good reasons to serve Christ at home. But here is a bad reason you need to make sure is not your reason: your instinct for self-preservation. There are plenty of things to be nervous about as you consider cross-cultural mission. But I suggest that you meditate on Psalm 91 and ask yourself whether your instinct for self-preservation is keeping you from stepping out of safety, with nothing but angels to hold you up.

Because here's the thing: nothing ventured, nothing gained, as they say. When you make God your refuge and start to live out your love for him as a protected person, you will begin to know the satisfaction that only comes from the God we learn to know on active service: the God who protects, who answers, who delivers, who honours and who saves. Praise be to him!

6

Psalm 118:
his love endures for ever

Psalm 118 is not even thirty verses long, but it looms over the book of Psalms like a mountain. I don't think there's any preparation for this psalm in what has come before. As far as I can see it is entirely new, a work of such profound and far-reaching imagination that it could only have come from God.

So perhaps it's not surprising that as I prepared these studies I struggled more with this psalm than any of the others. This is the only chapter in the book that I have rewritten since delivering it as a talk. Who knows, perhaps I shall rewrite it again one day. Every preacher must be willing to persevere over his or her task, to trust that God will sow the preached word into receptive hearts, but never to grow complacent with their efforts.

To do this psalm justice, we need to look over it twice. For the first half of our study we'll stay clear of the details and examine the psalm in broad strokes. Then we'll go back to the beginning and read more closely, as we move to consider the great revelation at the heart of this psalm: the glory of God displayed in the face of Christ.

Psalm 118: the big picture

Psalm 118 in its context

The first unique thing about Psalm 118 is its context. We don't know who wrote it (Calvin guessed it was David), but the author of the Psalms has chosen to use it as the centrepiece of a massive thanksgiving for the return from exile, which runs from Psalm 107 all the way to Psalm 136. (There are other ways of interpreting the structure of the long and complex fifth Book; this reading, which I find especially helpful, does not rule out all the others.[1])

You may remember that Book IV ended with a plea for the LORD to gather the people of Israel and rescue them from exile:

Save us, LORD our God,
   and gather us from the nations,
that we may give thanks to your holy name
   and glory in your praise.
(Psalm 106:47)

As Book V opens we see that prayer answered:

Let the redeemed of the LORD tell their story –
   those he redeemed from the hand of the foe,
those he gathered from the lands,
   from east and west, from north and south.
(Psalm 107:2)

Do you remember the three basic types of psalm? Lament for the dark times; praise for the bright times; and thanksgiving for the moments of transition. In the plot of the book of Psalms this is the *nation's* moment of transition, from exile to return, from death to life. And so Book V assembles thirty psalms, some of them very old, into a great drama of thanksgiving, like a play in three acts. Its theme is stated at the very beginning, in Psalm 107:1, and restated at the close, in Psalm 136:1:

Give thanks to the LORD, for he is good,
   his love endures for ever.

The only other statements of this theme come at the start and finish of Psalm 118, the midpoint of this great thanksgiving (see Figure 6).

Act 1 of this thanksgiving is the return of the king. After the failure of the monarchy in Book III, the king was absent from Book IV. But now we have a king again, and this time he's an ideal

	opening number	107	Refrain (107:1)
Act 1	**the return of the King**	108 – 110	
bridge	two praise acrostics	111 – 112	
Act 2	**the second exodus**	113 – 118	Refrain (118:1, 29)
interlude	law written on the heart	119	
Act 3	**the pilgrimage to Zion**	120 – 134	
	closing number	135 – 136	Refrain (136:1)

Figure 6 **The great thanksgiving drama of Book V**

King. In his weakness he shows perfect trust in God, so he is elevated to the right hand of God to finally fulfil the promise of Psalm 2, that he would rule the nations.

Act 2 is a group of six psalms that Jews call the Egyptian, or Passover, Hallel. These psalms are sung at family celebrations of the Passover, and Jesus sang them with his disciples at the last supper. They celebrate the exodus from Egypt as a great revelatory act. This is who God is (see Figure 7).

Who is the LORD of the exodus? (Psalms 113 – 118)	
• He raises up the lowly	113
• Creation trembles at his presence	114
• The gods of the nations are impotent before him	115
• He delivers his precious people from death	116
• All nations will see this and praise him	117
• All of the above!	118

Figure 7 **The Passover Hallel**

According to the Passover Hallel, the LORD of the exodus raises up the lowly; creation trembles at his presence; the gods of the nations are impotent before him as he delivers his precious people from death; all nations will see this and praise him.

So Psalm 118 is an exodus psalm – but an exodus psalm with a difference. As part of the great thanksgiving of Book V, Psalms 113 – 118 become a symbol of the return from exile. Isaiah first developed this idea of return from exile as a 'second exodus', and there are many links to Isaiah in these psalms. As we saw in

Psalm 91, God promised to replay the exodus to bring lowly Israel from death in Babylon, across the wilderness, and back to Mount Zion and life in the presence of God.

Psalm 118 ends act 2 with a procession to the temple, and in act 3 we see the procession up close. In the fifteen 'psalms of ascent' we see the ordinary people of the land – farmers, townsfolk – on pilgrimage to the temple, looking for God's protection and blessing through the ups and downs of daily life.

In between the Passover psalms and the pilgrim psalms we have the massive Psalm 119. This psalm is the key to Israel's future. Once the people are back in the land, what's to stop them turning away from God again, breaking the covenant again, losing everything? To prevent that, their hearts must be transformed, their desires must be shaped by God's word. Psalm 119 shows an individual who has the law written on his or her heart. It's the destination of the Passover psalms, and the starting-point for the pilgrim psalms.

So that's the context for Psalm 118: a great drama of thanksgiving for the return from exile, beginning with the return of the king, continuing with the second exodus of the nation, and ending with a pilgrimage to Zion and the temple. It's a drama that raises three important questions for us as we come to Psalm 118 itself. Just think for a moment about the implied actors of this drama. They are Jews returned from Babylon to the land, but without a king. So:

- *Question 1.* Who is the king act 1 celebrates?

- *Question 2.* If Psalm 91 has already presented the return from exile as a second exodus, and God's people have already returned, then what sort of exodus is act 2 imagining?

- *Question 3.* In act 3 the pilgrims look to Mount Zion for God's help. But the prophecies about Zion have not yet come true. When will the God enthroned in heaven rule the nations from Zion?

The return from exile in 586 BC was a wonderful fulfilment of prophecy, but only a partial fulfilment. The great thanksgiving drama anticipates its complete fulfilment. To figure out what 'complete fulfilment' looks like, we will need to answer those three questions:

1 Who is the king?
2 What sort of exodus should we expect?
3 When will God rule the nations from Zion?

A re-enactment

Imagine that you have just been in a football stadium watching a great contest play itself out in the arena. Your side scored a come-from-behind victory, and your heart is still racing from the experience – the roaring surf of sound from the booming crowd that lifted you from your seat for ninety minutes.

And now you're in a crowded pub, and noisy fans are reliving the match. They're watching a highlights reel and cheering, and then a few people clear some space and do a shot-by-shot re-enactment of each goal. What a night!

You know what I'd love to see one day? That scene in the pub translated into church on Resurrection Day. Because that's what Psalm 118 is: a noisy and dramatic re-enactment of Christ's resurrection.

We'll come to the resurrection later on. To start with, I want you simply to take in the rhetoric and the Irish-pub dynamics of the psalm (I've adapted the NIV slightly here):

²Let Israel say:
  his love endures for ever!
³Let the house of Aaron say:
  his love endures for ever!
⁴Let those who fear the LORD say:
  his love endures for ever!

Can you hear the call and response? The repetitions are like a football chant. The crowd is getting worked up, ramping up the energy, preparing for a big night.

Like a football game, Psalm 118 is a psalm of two halves (see Figure 8). In the first half we hear an individual re-enacting what I've called his exodus. It's like the person in the pub acting out the centre-forward's run through the defence and scoring of the winning goal. The hero of Psalm 118 tells the audience a three-part story of rescue, and a couple of times during the narrative the crowd gets to join in.

1	**The crowd cheers: 'His love endures for ever!'**	**1–4**
2	**An individual re-enacts his exodus**	**5–18**
	a dramatic rescue (+ four-line reflection)	5–9
	a dramatic victory (+ four-line reflection)	10–14
	a noisy celebration (+ four-line reflection)	15–18
3	**He completes his exodus; Israel welcomes him home**	**19–28**
	the victor's righteousness	19–21
	the crowd's insight	22–24
	a plea for victory	25
	a triumphal procession . . .	26–27
	. . . with the victor at its head	28
4	**The crowd cheers: 'His love endures for ever!'**	**29**

Figure 8 **The dramatic structure of Psalm 118**

But in verse 19 the scene changes and we find ourselves outside the temple with our hero knocking at the door. The people inside the temple reply, and he comes inside. In verse 22 the crowd then praises God for his amazing rescue of the hero, and in verse 26 everyone welomes the hero home and joins in a triumphal procession.

The second half of the psalm is sometimes called an 'entrance liturgy', because we have other examples of it, such as Psalm 24. So we think that this knocking-at-the-door-of-the-temple ritual was an actual ritual once upon a time. But the way it's incorporated into the hero's rescue story is something quite new. Nobody (in my opinion) has been able to come up with a convincing scenario for this psalm in Israel's history or in David's life.

I think we have to understand Psalm 118 as pure drama, a work of art, a prophecy to be performed in anticipation of the real thing. Jews after the return from exile could perform it in the reconstructed temple if they liked, but it could be performed anywhere, including in an upper room on the night before Jesus' death.

A re-enactment of the exodus

So there's the re-enactment. But what's the contest these cheering fans are celebrating? The exodus? The second exodus? Maybe a third? Before we turn to the details of the psalm, let's get the contest clear in our heads. Our starting-point is verse 1:

> ¹Give thanks to the Lord, for he is good;
>   his love endures for ever.

The Lord's *goodness* points to his good creation, and his *love* points to his gracious redemption of his people, supremely demonstrated in the exodus.

To redeem Israel, God had to defeat Pharaoh and his gods, the armies of Egypt and the nations, and the hostile waters of chaos – basically the whole creation risen in rebellion against its Maker. Put all those forces together and you could imagine the original exodus as the slaying of a vast monster, which held Israel captive in its lair.

The exile was different, because the people of Israel were being judged for their sin. Jeremiah imagines Babylon as a monster that gobbled Israel up like a sheep, dead. And his prediction of a second exodus from Babylon began with God slaying this monster, slitting it open and pulling Israel out – miraculously alive! (Jeremiah 50:17–20).

The slaying of the original exodus monster and the rescue of captive Israel was a world-changing act of power prompted by pity; the slaying of the Babylon monster and the resurrection of sinful Israel was a world-changing act of mercy prompted by love.

And yet, as we've seen, the return from Babylon was under-whelming. Yes, it was like a second exodus, and in a sense Israel came back from the dead, but where was the defeat of creation powers and the subduing of the nations? The Babylon monster was slain, but it turned out to be a baby monster. The monster God has to kill to accomplish the real second exodus is going to be much bigger. In fact, the biggest monster of all. And it's this final and climactic exodus that Psalm 118 anticipates.

The way it does this is by reaching back to the song the Israelites sang after they crossed the Red Sea. I want to lay that song alongside the psalm so you can appreciate what's going on.

Exodus 15 begins with the Red Sea crossing:

> I will sing to the LORD,
>   for he is highly exalted.
> Both horse and driver
>   he has hurled into the sea.
> (Exodus 15:1)

There are no close parallels yet, but you might notice that verses 5–7 of the psalm feel very similar, with rescue followed by triumph over the enemy.

The close parallels start in the next part of Exodus 15, which sings of the uniqueness of the LORD who saves:

> The LORD is my strength and my defence;
>   he has become my salvation . . .
> Your right hand, LORD,
>   was majestic in power.
> Your right hand, LORD,
>   shattered the enemy.
> (Exodus 15:2, 6)

Verse 14 of the psalm quotes Exodus 15:2, word for word. And in the next two verses of the psalm the actors pick up the repeated 'Your right hand, LORD' from Exodus 15:6. Whatever is going on in Psalm 118, this is not the baby monster of Babylon being defeated; this is the real deal, the conquest of rebellious creation so that Israel can be rescued and brought into the presence of God.

That journey to God's presence is the theme of the second half of both Exodus 15 and Psalm 118. In Exodus 15 the LORD who subdues the nations is celebrated, and the language of marvelling in verse 11 is echoed in verse 23 of the psalm:

Who among the gods
   is like you, LORD?
Who is like you –
   majestic in holiness,
awesome in glory,
   working wonders?
(Exodus 15:11)

The final part of Exodus 15 anticipates the LORD bringing the Israelites across the wilderness to Zion:

You will bring them in and plant them
   on the mountain of your inheritance –
the place, LORD, you made for your dwelling,
   the sanctuary, Lord, your hands established.
(Exodus 15:17)

This is the same journey the actors travel in Psalm 118, ending at the house of the LORD in verses 26 and 27.

So that's the contest Psalm 118 re-enacts. Not a football match re-enacted in a pub, but an exodus battle between the LORD and the hostile powers of creation, a contest for which his defeat of Babylon and its gods was just a practice match.

A re-enactment of the exodus, but without Israel

And this is the point where Psalm 118 does something truly unique and amazing, where it becomes a piece of Scripture without any real parallel in the Old Testament. It takes the story of God's redemption of Israel from Egypt, and removes Israel from the story. Israel's only role in the exodus story was to be rescued. Its people were slaves, entirely passive. But in Israel's place, Psalm 118 inserts a Hero. And no ordinary Hero. In verse 10 he speaks of cutting down the surrounding nations – which makes him a king.

The quotes from Exodus 15 treat the king's battles as though the enemy nations were the hostile waters of the Red Sea, and the king was the nation of Israel saved by God's right hand. The Exodus quotes make the king replace Israel.

And that fundamentally changes the exodus story. There's no king of Israel involved in either the exodus or the return from exile. And there's no Israel involved in this private royal exodus of Psalm 118. Instead, we have the returned King from act 1 of the thanksgiving drama.

In the context of Book V, the people opening the gate in verse 20 become Jews returned from exile. They have rebuilt the temple, but they don't have a king. And so they are performing a great drama to act out an event that hasn't happened yet: the arrival of God's exalted King. And they've made his arrival into a second exodus. It's as if they don't think the second exodus has really happened yet, even though they've returned from Babylon.

And this is where we leave our overview and turn to some details. The return from exile is unfinished. The predictions of the prophets are only partially fulfilled. To kill the monster and rescue Israel from the death of exile, God is going to need a Champion. A Hero.

The hero triumphs

A dramatic rescue (118:5–9)

We resume in verse 5, with a solo player re-enacting the hero's victorious run:

> 5When hard pressed, I cried to the LORD;
> he brought me into a spacious place.

'Hard pressed' suggests being trapped in a tight place, a narrow space. The word can be used for internal constriction – anxiety, depression; or for external oppression – enemies, sickness. Either way, as we've seen from earlier psalms, it is an experience of the encroachment of death into life. Like being buried alive. The hard-pressed King cries out to the LORD, and his cry is answered. He comes from a narrow place into a broad space. This feeling of broadening out is intensified by broadening out the two lines of verse 5 into four lines in verses 6 and 7:

> ⁶The LORD is with me; I will not be afraid.
>   What can mere mortals do to me?
> ⁷The LORD is with me; he is my helper.
>   I look in triumph on my enemies.

As he repeats 'The LORD is with me, the LORD is with me', the released person starts to uncoil: first he loses his fear, then his 'fear' transforms to a 'look' of triumph. All because of the LORD's presence. God is the only person the Psalms call a *helper*, and it basically means that without God you'd be dead. But with God, the King stands free and breathes.

Verses 8 and 9 take a step back and draw a moral from the King's rescue:

> ⁸It is better to take refuge in the LORD
>   than to trust in humans.
> ⁹It is better to take refuge in the LORD
>   than to trust in princes.

The change of tone makes me suspect that the crowd gets to say these lines. They've perceived a couple of things. First of all, no human power could have rescued the King; but when he looked to God for safety, like the faithful Israelite in Psalm 91, he became completely secure and confident. Second, the escalation from humans to princes hints, I think, at how different God's power is from that of humans. Princes in Israel's experience oppress the powerless; but the LORD's power helps the helpless.

A dramatic victory (118:10–14)

The King's rescue story was told subjectively, so we could feel his experience of claustrophobia and release. But now in verses 10–12 the camera steps back, and it's all action for the victory story:

¹⁰All the nations surrounded me,
    but in the name of the LORD I cut them down.
¹¹They surrounded me on every side,
    but in the name of the LORD I cut them down.
¹²They swarmed around me like bees,
    but they were consumed as quickly as burning thorns;
    in the name of the LORD I cut them down.

Once again there's an escalation across these lines: surrounded in verse 10; then doubly surrounded in verse 11; then an image of inhuman violence in verse 12; and then a whole extra line to describe the end result: a raging fire of opposition, but built of dry thorns that burn out almost at once.

Each wave of bad guys gets larger and more vicious, but the King's response never needs to change. 'In the name of the LORD' means that he fights as the LORD's representative, but also that he fights with the LORD's power. He speaks of it as if it's a weapon. First he raises his weapon for all to see: 'The name of the LORD'. In Hebrew there's an extra word of emphasis: 'Oh yeah!' Then the kill stroke: 'I cut them down!'

So, who's doing the cutting down? In the previous section the King seemed entirely passive, but not here. The way that the LORD and his Messiah work together against their enemies is very consistent in the Psalms. Remember Psalm 2:

I will make the nations your inheritance . . .
You will break them with a rod of iron . . .
(vv. 8–9)

Or Psalm 110:

The LORD will extend your mighty sceptre from Zion, saying,
    'Rule in the midst of your enemies!'
(v. 2)

The King is not like Israel. He fights the powers of chaos as they never could, and makes himself a living embodiment of the LORD's power.

In the four-line reflection contained in verses 13 and 14 the King doesn't deny his own active role, but he gives priority in everything to the LORD:

> ¹³I was pushed back and about to fall,
>   but the LORD helped me.
> ¹⁴The LORD is my strength and my defence;
>   he has become my salvation.

It was all God, all the way. Even the first line, 'I was pushed back', implies that it was the LORD doing the pushing. The LORD used the King's sufferings to reveal himself, to display his power over every other power, including death – and not just his power but also his regard for the lowly, his propensity to save.

A noisy celebration (118:15–18)

In the final scene of this exodus re-enactment the people speak a second time. Actually they yell, using words inspired by the Song of the Sea in Exodus 15:

> ¹⁵Shouts of joy and victory
>   resound in the tents of the righteous:
> 'The LORD's right hand has done mighty things!
>   ¹⁶The LORD's right hand is lifted high;
>   the LORD's right hand has done mighty things!'

They're praising the LORD, of course, but when they say 'right hand' they are describing the exalted King who wields God's power over death.

Let's stand with the people a moment and try to take in what's happened. We've witnessed the drama of a second exodus, which means that it concerns Israel, dead in exile because of sin, being returned to life in the land. But the exodus monster in this drama is not Babylon. It's Death itself, and killing Death is not as simple as kicking the legs from under Egypt's army and its gods, and karate-chopping the hostile waters of the Sea. It takes a Champion willing to be swallowed by the monster and, from deep inside that terrible place, to shred the monster's heart and slash his way out.

Verse 17 gives me goose bumps sometimes. The King stands astride the carcass of Death, the Name of the LORD bloody in his hands, and utters this statement of destiny:

'I will not die but live.'

He's not just talking about this moment of victory. He's talking about for ever. He's talking about a life of endless praise:

> [17]I will not die but live,
>   and will proclaim what the LORD has done.

It was the LORD who got him into the monster, and the LORD who got him out. What verse 13 hinted at is clear in verse 18. God stands on both sides of death:

> [18]The LORD has chastened me severely,
>   but he has not given me over to death.

God is sovereign over the King's suffering *and* his victory. And life was always God's purpose for his suffering. God was using the powers of death as tools to transform a dying life into a praising life.

I believe Psalm 118 gives us a bold image of Jesus after his crucifixion fighting free of the power of death in the name of the LORD. Now of course the New Testament is very clear that *God* raised Jesus from the dead. If you could raise yourself from death it wouldn't be death. And yet the resurrection was not a drama in which Jesus was passive. The LORD's right hand was extended to Jesus in death, to use as a weapon. Peter's statement on the day of Pentecost is thought-provoking: 'God raised him from the dead ... because it was impossible for death to keep its hold on him' (Acts 2:24). Behind this lies Jesus' own remarkable statement:

> The reason my Father loves me is that I lay down my life – only to take it up again. No one takes it from me, but I lay it down of

my own accord. I have authority to lay it down and authority to take it up again. This command I received from my Father. (John 10:17–18)

Now these are deep mysteries, largely hidden from us, but in the first half of this psalm I believe we have a prophetic picture of the hidden drama of Easter Saturday, a spiritual battle and momentous victory, which God's people are re-enacting in these verses with shouts of joy and acclamation.

The hero is honoured

The hero returns (118:19–21)

In the second half of the drama the hero returns from his ordeal, and rejoins the people he fought to save. I've been ignoring the people so we can focus on the King's battle. But there have been plenty of clues that his salvation is also their salvation. Just the fact that the King has undergone an exodus is enough to show that he's standing in for Israel. And then there's the chastening of the King in verse 18. 'Chastisement' means a harsh rebuke aimed at steering someone back on track, as if the King were a rebel to be punished. The King has shown nothing but trust, but if Israel's death in Babylon was a punishment for the people's crimes, then their Champion needs to share that punishment so that he can truly represent them. It's no wonder they've been so excited by the battle!

In verse 19 the King stands at the door, and the people open it for him in verse 20:

> ¹⁹Open for me the gates of the righteous;
>   I will enter and give thanks to the LORD.
> ²⁰This is the gate of the LORD
>   through which the righteous may enter.

The King's arrival changes everything. In verse 19 the word 'righteous' is singular. But when the righteous one has entered, the way is open for others too. In verse 20 the word 'righteous' is plural.

What does it mean to be righteous? It means to relate rightly, and the King's words of thanks in verse 21 illustrate this perfectly:

> ²¹I will give you thanks, for you answered me;
>   you have become my salvation.

The King related rightly to God by asking him for help and trusting him; God related rightly to the King by saving him; and now the King relates rightly to God by thanking him. A person who is rightly related to the LORD comes to experience him as Saviour.

The people honour him (118:22–24)

One of the lovely dynamics of this part of the drama is that after his request for entry the King only ever speaks to the LORD, and all he ever says is 'thank you'. But his presence galvanizes the people. It gives them a real speaking part. And they, too, use their voice to say 'thank you', to praise both God and his King:

> ²²The stone the builders rejected
>   has become the cornerstone;
> ²³the LORD has done this,
>   and it is marvellous in our eyes.
> ²⁴The LORD has done it this very day;
>   let us rejoice today and be glad.

The people's speech in verse 22 is among the best-known lines in the Psalms because of the way Jesus applied it to himself (e.g. Matthew 21:42). We know that Jesus is 'the living Stone – rejected by humans but chosen by God', as Peter puts it (1 Peter 2:4). But let's take a minute to consider the saying here in its original context.

The people are making a theological observation about the drama of verses 5–18, in what sounds like a proverb or saying. At its most basic it's pointing out that the King is a very unlikely candidate for greatness. He is weak, hard pressed, chastened – quite the wrong shape and size to be made the centre and reference-point for the whole building. When the people call this marvellous and say 'The LORD has done it' they are alluding to the exodus and to their shouts of joy back in verse 15. They are saying that God's ultimate exodus miracle was to lift a man like this from death to greatness.

In the logic of the psalm, 'the builders' don't refer to anyone specific. It's just a way of saying that this is a stone that doesn't measure up, a stone a builder would never use. But the building, I think, does represent something. Remember where these words are being spoken. As the King enters the temple court, the people gathered inside compare him to the cornerstone in the building behind them. To identify the building as the temple makes sense of the whole psalm. Because if the King is made the *temple's* cornerstone, it means that his death and resurrection are a revelation to the world of God himself.

The temple was the place where heaven and earth met, where God came to dwell in holy splendour and to rule his creation. But now God has done something new. He has raised his chastised and unsplendid King from death, and made him the reference-point by which the creation will now understand what God's glory and holiness and greatness look like. The King emerges from the carcass of death, knocks on the gate, enters the dwelling of God, becomes its cornerstone . . . and all at once God is revealed in never-before-imagined splendour.

Verse 24 has traditionally been used by the church on Resurrection Day in the form:

This is the day the LORD has made,
let us rejoice and be glad in it!

The NIV is a more accurate translation, and strictly speaking we rejoice in what God did on that day. But the tradition is not wrong. Easter Day is special because when Jesus rose from the dead, the true nature of God suddenly became marvellously clear. As Paul explains in Philippians, Christ's act of self-emptying and obedience to death was an act in which God manifested his divine nature more gloriously than in anything else he had ever done, and so God took Jesus from death and lifted him up for the world to gaze upon him in awe, and finally recognize what it means for God to be God (Philippians 2:5–11).

We celebrate Christ's resurrection not because it demonstrates God's power to raise the dead (we already knew he could do that), but because it vindicates Christ's weakness, his trusting self-sacrifice, as the true power and glory of God.

The hero is followed

The actors break the fourth wall (118:25)

Verse 25 is the most passionate verse in the psalm:

> ²⁵LORD, save us!
> LORD, grant us success!

These are very intense lines, like music moving up into a higher key with added trumpets. Why such intensity? Remember that this a drama about something that hasn't happened yet. And this is where the people pause their drama to call on God to complete the work he began when he brought them back from exile. 'Success' means a life that prospers; it implies freedom from external threats. The people are imagining a world like the one in Psalm 117, where God's rule extends over the nations.

Placing this prayer into their praise of the risen King makes it a prayer of confidence rather than desperation. By Jesus' time, 'save us' had morphed from a prayer into an Aramaic shout of praise: 'Hosanna!' But in Psalm 118 it is still a prayer, albeit a confident one.

The hero leads his people to journey's end (118:26–29)

In the final scene of this prophetic drama the King completes his journey: through the gates, into the temple and now all the way to the altar, with the crowd first blessing him and then forming a festive procession. If you look carefully, you'll see that the crowd blesses the King and the LORD together, as one:

> 26Blessed is he who comes in the name of the LORD.
> From the house of the LORD we bless you.

'He who comes in the name of the LORD' picks up the imagery of the King wielding God's name in a joint action against death. And when the people say 'we bless you', it's a plural 'you', as the NIV footnote points out. When they look at the King, they see the LORD.

In the next verse they reverse their blessing:

> 27The LORD is God,
> and he has made his light shine on us.

The LORD is God. There is no other. The King's journey has relegated every other god to the dust-heap. The visible light that shines on the people from the invisible God is, I think, the King. It reminds me of the moment when Jesus stepped into his public ministry, and Matthew quotes these words from Isaiah:

> on those living in the land of the shadow of death
> a light has dawned.
> (Matthew 4:16)

This is the King whose journey through Death will make him the shining manifestation of the glory of God.

The King's journey to life only ends when he stands before God and praises him – because life without praise is not real life. To live is to praise. And for the last short leg of his journey he brings the people along with him. They've been waiting in the temple courts for his arrival, but now they can make the final journey to the altar because they have their King to go before them and lead their praises:

> With boughs in hand, join in the festal procession
> up to the horns of the altar.

²⁸You are my God, and I will praise you;
   you are my God, and I will exalt you.

(The second half of verse 27 is difficult, because the Hebrew word for 'boughs' is the same as the word for 'ropes'. I prefer the meaning the NIV has chosen to the alternative in the footnote, but the point remains the same either way.)

Psalm 118 as the centre of the great thanksgiving of Book V

Before we reflect on the fulfilment of this second half of the psalm in the life of Jesus, let's remind ourselves of the context of the great thanksgiving in Psalms 107 – 136 with its three acts: the return of the king, the second exodus and the pilgrimage to Zion.

Psalm 118 has given us some answers to the questions that surrounded each of those topics.

- *1 Who is the coming king?* He will be an exalted Messiah whose weakness and trust conquers death and makes him a living embodiment of the glory of God.

- *2 What sort of exodus should we expect?* A victory over the rebellious powers of creation, a deliverance from the great monster Death, and a liberation from sin into a life of praise.

- *3 When will God rule the nations from Zion?* The moment the triumphant King comes to his temple, God's light of salvation will shine on his people and answer their prayer for security from every enemy.

But Psalm 118 goes even further. As it explores the relationship between God and the King, it points us to a key truth, a truth that sometimes gets lost in all the excitement of victory. And this truth brings us one more time to the Lord Jesus.

Jesus our hero

The meaning of Palm Sunday

Remember how the psalm starts and finishes: with a call to thank God for his goodness and love in bringing Israel back from exile. But Israel's exile would not be truly over until Christ rose from the dead.

As Jesus rode into Jerusalem as its King, the crowd acted out Psalm 118 ahead of him. Men and women spread branches on the road and shouted:

'Hosanna to the Son of David!'

'Blessed is he who comes in the name of the Lord!'

'Hosanna in the highest heaven!'
(Matthew 21:9)

The people in the crowd on Palm Sunday did not understand the Scriptures. They had no clue what it meant to be God's King. They thought that Jesus was coming to take power and to elevate them all to the power and glory they craved. But when Jesus arrived at the temple and dismounted from his donkey, he entered (without knocking) and drove out the idolaters (Matthew 21:12). He lifted up the lowly from death: the lame and the blind (Matthew 21:14). He brought down the powerful and the proud: the wicked tenants of God's vineyard (Matthew 21:33). And the crowd saw him killed for it.

It turns out that what the people were actually doing on that first Palm Sunday was ushering the hero onto the battlefield where the monster waited. And that monster was them. The same people who had cried 'Hosanna' now surrounded Jesus like the hostile waters of the Red Sea. God used them as his unwitting instruments to chastise his Son in their stead.

And yet, God brilliantly used their actions to fulfil Scripture. Because it was precisely in his humiliation and death that God's

King demonstrated what true power and glory look like. On Good Friday the people thought they had fixed a mistake, but by crucifying the Lord they were placing him on the road to glory. The destination of that road was the right hand of God, and it was at Jesus' resurrection that the people's shout, 'Blessed is he who comes in the name of the LORD,' found its reply.

God's power is made perfect in weakness

And this is the deep truth of Psalm 118, the truth it reveals by showing us that the stone the builders rejected is the very light that shines from God. God does not show his power by making the King great and powerful. He shows his power in the King's weakness and trust – not just *through* his weakness, but *in* it.

In the first half of the psalm we saw Jesus the hero fighting free of death. But he did it in the name of the LORD, not in his own strength. In the second half of the psalm we saw Jesus risen and triumphant, shining upon his people with the light of God. But his glory was the glory of a rejected stone. Let me repeat what I said a moment ago: we celebrate Christ's resurrection not because it demonstrates God's power to raise the dead, but because it proves that Christ's trusting self-sacrifice is the true power and glory of God.

This is a mystery that turns human ideas of power upside down. We define power as a sustained exertion of force that gets work done. The more force you exert, and the more quickly you exert it, the bigger the change you make to the world. This is how things work both in the physical world and in the human world, whether in economics, politics or personal relationships.

But God works – on a scale we cannot even imagine – using weakness, not strength. Not that God is weak, of course. His power is manifest in the universe he creates with a word, effortlessly. No power in heaven or on earth can shake his sovereignty. And yet the LORD does not manhandle his creation, as though he were a human being. His mysterious presence carries a power that has nothing to do with power as we understand it. God's power is nothing less than the visible outworking of the love that flows eternally between Father,

Son and Holy Spirit – a love that looks to us like weakness. Do you remember what Paul says about Christ's weakness?

> We preach Christ crucified: a stumbling-block to Jews and fool-ishness to Gentiles, but to those whom God has called, both Jews and Greeks, Christ the power of God and the wisdom of God. For the foolishness of God is wiser than human wisdom, and the weakness of God is stronger than human strength.
> (1 Corinthans 1:23–25)

If God's power was made perfect in Christ's weakness, why should his people expect to be strong?

We were saved in weakness. Like Israel, we, too, stand on both sides of the King's ordeal. Our rebellion and wickedness swarm around him like bees; our pride and self-regard drive him into the grave. But after he cuts down Death with the Name of the LORD, he turns towards us, holding salvation in his hands, and invites us to share it with him, to enter joyfully as righteous men and women through the gate of the LORD.

We serve in weakness. Do not make the same mistake as the Palm Sunday crowd, and imagine that Jesus' triumph over death liberates us into a life of triumph and conquest. Our strength is the Lord's mighty power, made perfect in our weakness. And so our weapons are prayer, truth, trust and the gospel of peace.

We rejoice in weakness. The King's trust was matched by the LORD's trustworthiness. As God reached down in love to rescue his King, the King's love for God blossomed into praise. As Jesus ascended to the Father, I like to think that he was singing these words:

> You are my God, and I will praise you;
> you are my God, and I will exalt you.
> I give thanks to you, LORD, for you are good;
> your love endures for ever.

7

Psalm 147:
what your breath is for

We are coming to the end of our journey through the Psalms. The starting-point for our final study is Psalm 118, because it teaches us that Christ's people can take hold of his destiny for themselves. 'I will not die but live.' At its most fundamental, that describes what it means to be human: not to die, but to live. The return of our bodies to the dust from which they came is an abomination and defilement of our humanity. It is not what we are for. We are made for life. But what is life? According to the Psalms, life is proclaiming what the LORD has done. If for a hundred years you ate, slept, worked, loved – if you changed the world! – but did not praise God, you never lived. Praise is what your breath is for. And praise is where the journey of this most wonderful of books finishes.

The end of the journey

The return of the King (Psalms 138 – 145)

Books I and II of the Psalms played out against the backdrop of the historical King David as he suffered, trusted, repented, gave thanks and sang hymns of praise. In Book III we saw the failure of the Davidic monarchy and the fall of the nation, and in Book IV we saw a kingless Israel in exile, singing for joy that the LORD reigns over the nations, but praying at the same time for the fulfilment of God's ancient promise to Abraham. When we reached Book V we saw a people rejoicing in the God who had brought them back from exile, and boldly anticipating the return of the King in a second exodus that would finally complete their journey back to the presence of God.

The people's prayers are finally answered in Psalms 138 – 145, which is the first block of Davidic psalms since Psalm 70. The king has returned, and he is now an ideal King who rejects evildoers, upholds the lowly and turns from sin. Yet he still suffers and laments and clings to God, and his journey ends with deep thanksgiving for God's faithfulness in all his trials, and a joyous call to every creature on earth to praise God's holy name for ever.

The return of the King is a great way to end the story of the Psalms. As Tolkien knew when he famously used the phrase for the third volume of his trilogy, it's how the history of our world will end too.[1] But why is the King still so weak? Psalm 2 led us to expect an exalted Son reigning in triumph at the LORD's right hand, so why not make Psalm 110 the final psalm? Why is the King at his return still not freed from travelling David's hard road? It seems a complicated way for God to bring about the fulfilment of his plan, an unnecessary embrace of hardship and suffering. Why, for that matter, does the risen Christ in the book of Revelation still look like a Lamb that was slain?

The book of Psalms gives a one-word answer to these questions: praise. Praise is the king's destination, as it is ours, and it is the journey that creates the destination.

Praise, the goal of everything (Psalms 146 – 150)

Many years ago my wife and I were on holiday in the Alps, and we rode a cable-car up to a spire of rock called the Aiguille du Midi, from which you can see all the way across to Mont Blanc. We could just make out a line of black specks toiling across the glacier towards the summit, and we could also see a helicopter headed in the same direction. You can be dropped off three hours from the summit if you have enough money to pay for it. Now if you were one of those climbers and you finally made the summit, would you resent the wealthy tourists who strolled up with their day packs? I don't think so. You'd feel sorry for them, wouldn't you? How pale and anaemic their enjoyment must be when set against the exhilaration of your achievement, the experience of grappling with the elements and the limits of your endurance! You feel reborn into a newly discovered world, you have a glow of joy and fulfilment – at least until you descend back to sea level.

The praise we sing is the result of the journey we have travelled. Why does the Messiah travel such a hard journey? Because of the praise that lies at its end.

The final five psalms each begin and end with 'Hallelujah', or in English, 'Praise the LORD'. Their praise expands out from a single individual to all Israel to all of creation, and as it does, the people of Israel emerge with a special role in God's purposes. By their praise they will bring the nations to bow before the LORD, and, at the end of all things, all things will be caught up into a feast of praise that never ends (see Figure 9).

Expanding circles of praise (Psalms 146 – 150)	
• My soul, praise the LORD!	146
• All Israel, praise the LORD!	147
• All creation, praise the LORD! Israel, you have a special role.	148
• Israel, may your praises bring creation under the LORD's rule!	149
• In the end, everything with breath will praise the LORD.	150

Figure 9 **The concluding Hallel**

The art of praise

Psalm 147 is organized around three commands to praise, in verses 1, 7 and 12. Each section alternates between praise of the Redeemer and praise of the Creator. It's jubilant from start to finish. The rhythms are regular and confident; there is none of the tension and release you get in a narrative. It's just pure praise.

We're all familiar with praise, because it's a basic and universal human response to things we admire. It may be the school kid who gives you every imaginable statistic about their sporting hero; or your friend who can't stop going on about this amazing girl he's started dating; or a new mum who wants you to admire a hundred apparently identical photos of her baby. When we praise something, we pay close attention to it and then we speak about it. In church we often sing praise, but most praise in life is simply spoken. All praise is enthusiastic, but what separates great praise from mediocre praise is not enthusiasm. It's detail. Praise rests on the art of noticing things.

The American poet Edward Hirsch suggests that the greatest poets of praise have been people 'who understood the piling up of particulars as a joyous poetic activity, who claimed the world by chanting its various names and delivering canticles of blessing upon it'.[2] The praise of God is no different. We need to give God the careful attention that praise gives to its subjects, because if we don't take the trouble to notice carefully, the truths we repeat week by week will slide into cliché. Our prayers and songs will have emotion without substance, and our knowledge of God will lose its conviction and its power. When we get used to God we have a problem.

You could think of Psalm 147 as a photo album in which the poet has collected some of the favourite things he's noticed about God. He does two things with these photos, things that are both typical of praise. First, he makes us look twice at each photo. In the first line of each poetic couplet he holds something up for our inspection, and then in the second line he pushes it towards us by saying something more specific or vivid or dramatic. And second, he arranges his photos carefully so that the combinations reveal new things about God that individual photos don't show.

Praise the transcendent Creator

Transcendence (147:1–6)

The first page of the album, verses 1–6, begins with a reminder of what we all know:

> [1]How good it is to sing praises to our God,
>   how pleasant and fitting to praise him!

The word translated 'sing praises' is used again in verse 7 to describe harp playing. Music, whether vocal or instrumental, is a gift from God, a wondrous property of created things that they vibrate and sing, and set our hearts vibrating in sympathy. Music lets us know we are alive, and draws us into the life around us. The power music can exert over the senses has made Christians from earliest times nervous about its uses, but the fact it's open to abuse doesn't stop it from being 'fitting' to praise God with. Why do you think God invented music in the first place? It aligns our hearts with one another; it stirs up our love for him; it reminds us how much we want to please him.

The photos we're about to look at in the rest of this psalm are photos best projected onto your imagination to the accompaniment of a stirring soundtrack. Perhaps you could try reading a psalm aloud that way in church some time. For now, we'll do what we can without music. Here is the first photo:

> ²The LORD builds up Jerusalem;
>> he gathers the exiles of Israel.
> ³He heals the broken-hearted
>> and binds up their wounds.

This is not praising the LORD for his act of bringing Israel back from exile; it's praising him for being the sort of God who would do that. You want to know who our God is? Watch him build his city. No – really watch; see how he does it using a bunch of rejected stones, how he shapes outcasts into his dwelling on earth. Now come closer so we can get a good view of his chosen people. 'Broken hearts' are what we would call broken spirits – those without the will to carry on. And the bandaging of wounds is, I think, a metaphor for the repair of emotional hurts.

There is obviously a story behind this photo, but the photo is not about the story. It's about the subject. 'If you want to know who the LORD is, watch him heal a broken heart,' says the poet. 'Look at that – that's my God right there!'

Here is the second photo:

> ⁴He determines the number of the stars
>> and calls them each by name.
> ⁵Great is our Lord and mighty in power;
>> his understanding has no limit.

Quite a contrast to the first photo, isn't it? Counting the stars is the impossible challenge God gave Abraham to help him grasp just how many people would one day trace their faith back to him. But nothing is impossible with God. And when you look closer, you see him naming each star. In Israel's world, just as in some cultures today, the stars were feared and worshipped; priests consulted them for their ominous significance. To name a thing is to make it yours, to control it, and this photo relegates each star to the status of God's creature. When the people of Israel looked at the stars they saw something just as awesome but radically different from what the pagans saw. They saw one God, Creator of all, his sheer scale and vastness unfathomable.

But look closer and you'll see the truly amazing feature for which this photo was chosen: the power of his understanding. The word 'number' at the beginning of verse 4 is the same word translated 'limit' at the end of verse 5. The poet is playing with words to help us appreciate something amazing.

We're impressed by physical size and power because we can see and feel it. But what we should really be impressed by is the intelligence that put each star in position, gave each subatomic particle its place in the vast moving web of being, and sustained it over millennia of time in a grand and beautiful ballet of praise. *That* is who our God is.

A study in contrasts

The poet has also chosen these two photos to see what we can notice about God when we lay them side by side. We see the tender compassion of the One who forgives our sins, who heals our broken hearts. And then we are reminded who he *really* is.

I knew an eminent Cambridge professor, a world expert in his field, who used to teach Sunday school children in a small village church. Those seven-year-olds had no conception of who he really was, let alone the gulf between his knowledge and theirs. They simply knew him as a kind old man who loved them.

Here we have a photo of the unimaginably glorious Lord of time, space and human destiny. And yet. This transcendent Creator interests himself in banished exiles, in the likes of you and me. Verse 6 is a combination of both photos:

⁶The LORD sustains the humble
 but casts the wicked to the ground.

Its first line is an echo of the first line of verse 2. In Hebrew they are identically constructed, they rhyme, and they use God's name, the LORD. The second line links back to verse 4 by completing a journey from 'the stars' to 'the ground'.

This is a side-point, but I want you to notice that the composer of this song didn't just throw words together as he felt led. This is a poem that has been constructed with all the art and skill the poet could bring to it, to create something beautiful and fitting for the praise of God.

But there's something else going on in the poet's plan beyond a simple study in contrasts. Verse 6 is not just a combination of the photos; it also follows on from the second one. We've had a glimpse of God's transcendent wisdom. But what does that wisdom look like in practice? Helping up the humble. The Creator chooses to redeem his exiles, to build his church with broken people, because this act of redemption will complete his creation.

Perhaps the God we experience as Saviour is not like the Cambridge professor speaking kindly and simply for children. Perhaps making people alive who were dead in their sins is the most transcendent and wise thing he has ever done. The destiny of the universe is fulfilled in the rescue of the lost. Praise the LORD!

Praise the benevolent Sustainer

Benevolence (147:7–11)

The second page of photos is prefaced by a second exhortation to sing and make music (verse 7). The photos themselves are comparisons rather than contrasts. The first image has three lines, because it's a little story rather than a standard photo:

⁸He covers the sky with clouds;
    he supplies the earth with rain
    and makes grass grow on the hills.

The story moves from heaven to earth, without tension or conflict. Its God feels a little closer to home than the Namer of the Stars. In Israel's day, people thought each zone of creation had its own gods. But in Israel's photo album, the God who determines human destiny is the same God who turns the hills green with spring rains. In Judea the high country is the grassy country, so this is very much a photo of the One who puts food on Israelite tables.

So I love the artistic decision *not* to make the next photo one of people eating together. Instead, verse 9 shows us animals and birds being fed by God:

⁹He provides food for the cattle
    and for the young ravens when they call.

God provides for every creature he created. We humans may be special, but he doesn't feed us *because* we are special. He feeds us because of who he is: the benevolent Sustainer who delights in making all things grow and flourish.

My favourite detail in this image is the ravens. Ravens were not only unclean according to the law, but everyone hated them. They are scavengers, and they prey upon smaller animals. Would you care for the young of such an animal? Yet their chicks in this photo are 'calling', which is the psalmist's regular word for prayer. There's no parent bird in the picture. God is their loving Parent, and he answers them when they cry to him. It's a lovely photo of God's mercy as provider. From his transcendent place above the heavens he hears a single hungry little 'caw!' and responds in compassion.

The God in these images is powerful, competent, generous, kind. But the final photo in this set adds another dimension to his character. It's something we haven't seen in this psalm before, and that's a God with a big grin on his face, a God who appears *delighted*.

Verses 10 and 11 stand at the very centre of the psalm, and I don't think that's an accident. Verse 10 has the psalm's longest lines, and feels like a proverb:

> [10]His pleasure is not in the strength of the horse,
>   nor his delight in the legs of the warrior;
> [11]the LORD delights in those who fear him,
>   who put their hope in his unfailing love.

The horse and the warrior are close parallels. The rippling muscles of a war-horse, its explosive acceleration, so impressive! And then the elite human athlete. People didn't build up muscly thighs to lift weights or win the Tour de France back then; the ultimate test of strength was the battlefield, where heroes were born. But this photo shows us that the Maker values different things, different features of what he's made, than we do. Why would strength and agility impress the One whose power and understanding has no limits? The delight we get from our sporting heroes, the pleasure they bring us, is the exact delight and pleasure the LORD takes in weak things that trust him – that recognize his awesome power, and cry out to him like baby ravens, because they know that their weakness and unattractiveness can never stop him from loving them.

You can tell God-fearers by their hope. Hope, not as in a feeling that things will get better, but hope as in *expectant waiting*. Hope as my dog hopes when she sits by our dinner table, watching us eat. Or, as Psalm 123 puts it:

> As the eyes of slaves look to the hand of their master,
>   as the eyes of a female slave look to the hand of her mistress,
> so our eyes look to the LORD our God,
>   till he shows us his mercy.
> (Psalm 123:2)

When God sees someone like that, he's filled with the same delight and pleasure that we feel when we see a sporting hero. Praise the LORD!

The power of hope

Psalm 147 points us to three truths about hope.

Christian hope can be a form of praise

Hope and praise are fundamentally similar because they are both activated by paying attention. When we look expectantly to God for help, we are fixing him clearly in our minds. And if that vision of God brings us joy, then hope becomes a form of praise.

Christian hope rests on a certainty, not a possibility

Former US president Barack Obama rose to fame on a speech dubbed 'The Audacity of Hope', a speech on the way hope can move people with few resources to work towards the possibility of a better world.[3] In a democracy you hope that enough people will join you and that vested interests won't be able to stop you. It's worth a punt, and hope will keep you soldiering through disappointments, because there's a glorious vision and it is a vision of the possible.

But the hope of Israel, the hope of the church, is hope in a certainty, because of God's 'unfailing love' (v. 11). That expression describes the love that stands behind God's promise to bless his people at all costs – ultimately, at the cost of his Son. And as we wait for what was promised, the Creator directs his creation to provide for us.

Christian hope has a unique power

Christian hope has one power that no other hope can lay claim to. It has the power to delight God. There is a lot of pain behind the praises of this psalm. God's beautiful creation marred by violence, his people judged, despised, persecuted . . . and out of all that pain and dirt a fragile and beautiful flower grows: the hope of God's people. And you'd better believe that he will nurture and cherish those flowers of hope wherever he finds them. The praises of God's hidden saints in Afghanistan will prevail over the most determined of enemies. The hope of God's suffering people in Somalia is more precious to him than diamonds.

Praise the LORD whose ways are hidden

As we move into the final part of the psalm, we take with us two portraits of the LORD: a transcendent Creator who redeems his broken people, because redemption completes creation; and a benevolent Sustainer who ensures that while the redeemed wait for him they are supplied with what they need from his creation.

The rebuilding of Jerusalem (147:12–14)

The final page of photos notices how mysteriously God completes his work and realizes our hope. In verses 12–14 the poet speaks directly to the city, beginning with a third call to praise:

> ^{12}Extol the LORD, Jerusalem;
>   praise your God, Zion.
>
> ^{13}He strengthens the bars of your gates
>   and blesses your people within you.
> ^{14}He grants peace to your borders
>   and satisfies you with the finest of wheat.

The rest of the psalm admires God's attributes, his ongoing behaviour. Verse 13 is the only photo that looks at a specific achievement. The language of strengthening gates and bars is particular to Nehemiah, so we can be reasonably confident that this is a photo of his successful reconstruction of the city in the face of stiff opposition. Nehemiah's prayers are a great example of the young raven crying out for physical provision to its heavenly Father. Obviously the wheat was grown in the countryside, so this photo is an example of the way God brings peace to the whole land, with Zion at its focus.

'Peace', or *shalom* in Hebrew, means that everything is 'as it should be', that it reflects the good order of creation. An absence of war and strife is obviously part of that, but so is good rain, rich harvests and a well-governed people.

The LORD is a God of peace, but the chequered history of Jerusalem doesn't seem like the greatest of examples. There's a bit of tension, isn't there, between the optimism of Nehemiah's achievement and the tragedy of the city of David, which God's people thought was impregnable before their outrageous behaviour led to its destruction. The psalm began with a photo that had broken-hearted exiles in the background; now we have a snapshot of blessed people in a protected city.

The mystery of God's ways (147:15–18)

As I said at the start, this is not a psalm about tension and plot; but the contrast between these two photos of Jerusalem sets the poet thinking about the mystery of God's ways. His final set of creation photos is all about mystery and wonder. He doesn't start them on a new page. He just leaves a little space and pastes them right under the Jerusalem photo. Verses 15–18 contain a wonderful passage:

> [15]He sends his command to the earth;
>   his word runs swiftly.
> [16]He spreads the snow like wool
>   and scatters the frost like ashes.
> [17]He hurls down hail like pebbles.
>   Who can withstand his icy blast?
> [18]He sends his word and melts them;
>   he stirs up his breezes, and the waters flow.

It's full of poetic and unusual language, as if God's transcendent wisdom is baked into the words. Its focus is weather events that were rare to Israelites, and which played no discernible role in the sustaining of creation. Life needs food, shelter, warmth. Frost and ice are not helpful!

But – I love this detail – these exotic phenomena are as familiar to God as our everyday home comforts. He uses his ice and cold as domestic objects with which to cover the world as effortlessly and casually as a person pulling on a sweater, or stirring the embers of a fire, or throwing crumbs for the birds. (The NIV has 'pebbles', which works OK, but I think 'breadcrumbs' is a better translation.) Verse 17 puts some humans into the frame for scale. Like one of those movies where people are shrunk down to a centimetre high, God's cosy domestic activities create a life-threatening drama for us.

But there's more going on in this photo. The poet takes this sense of mystery, the strangeness of the snow and frost, and puts it inside two references to God's word in verses 15 and 18. The juxtaposition alerts us to two kinds of mystery in God's word.

The first is the way God's word of command travels down from the highest heaven and runs around doing things for him. Verse 16 says that God spreads the snow, but his word is the thing doing the spreading. I don't think the poet thinks of the word as a person (we have to be careful not to read too much into this image), but he certainly understands that by his word the transcendent God makes himself mysteriously present among us.

The second thing the word does, in verse 18, is reverse the effects of its actions by melting the snow God scattered. I think we're supposed to apply this to Jerusalem. God draws near to his city and tears it down. Then he draws near and builds it up. We can see immediate causes for this. Babylon tore it down; Nehemiah built it up. And we can discern secondary causes. Israel's sin tore it down; Nehemiah's prayers built it up. But the ultimate causes are hidden. Why did God choose to create a history for the universe in which he tore down his city and built it up again? It's a mystery, and the psalm marvels and wonders at the strange magnificence of God's ways.

The mystery of God's word (147:19–20)

The final photo brings the mystery of the snow and ice right down into the lives of his people, by showing us that the word God speaks to freeze and thaw the world he also speaks to Israel, and the form that word takes when Israel hears it is not snow, but law:

> ¹⁹ He has revealed his word to Jacob,
>   his laws and decrees to Israel.
> ²⁰ He has done this for no other nation;
>   they do not know his laws.

Praise the LORD.

Verse 19 describes the law of Moses. You may remember from Psalm 1 that the path of the righteous is the path of meditation on the law. For Christians, that means the path of meditation on Scripture and obedience to Christ. And the final detail that fills the poet with praise is that this path has been revealed exclusively to his people. He's not excited in verse 20 because the nations are ignorant of God's path; he's excited because God's people are uniquely blessed. This is the token of the LORD's exclusive love, the love for which we can wait so confidently.

Before we close the album we need to examine verses 12–20 as a set of photos. They make a sandwich, with 'Rebuilt Zion' and 'The path of obedience' being the bread, and 'The mysterious word' making up the filling. It seems as if the poet is displaying the blessing of Zion as the destination of the path of obedience; but the route that path follows is mysterious and winding.

As we've walked together through the Psalms, we've traced Israel's tortuous journey, a journey that passed through rebellion and destruction, death and exile, before eventually the king was installed in Zion to rule the nations in fulfilment of the promise of Psalm 2. Now on the one hand it's true to say that this happened because the people of Israel strayed from God's path. But on the other hand, their disobedience created the circumstances for the King to destroy death and show the world that God's power is made perfect in weakness. It was all part of God's plan, but it made the King's path of obedience dark, winding and mysterious.

We should not expect our own paths to be any less winding or mysterious than his. The one thing that is not a mystery is how we should live. In case you've forgotten Psalm 1, let me remind you of the answer: walk his way!

The path of obedience

Psalm 147 points us to three truths about the path of obedience.

The path of obedience does not easily build the church

The 'photos' of Jerusalem, destroyed and rebuilt, remind us that the path of obedience is difficult and mysterious. Following it does not insulate us against loss. It makes us fools in the eyes of the world. It is a path from which we often stray. The church God builds with broken stones is unimpressive, slow to grow and quick to be corrupted. This is mysterious to us, but not to our transcendent God. He builds his church with the practised ease of someone pulling on a sweater.

Here is some wisdom from this psalm for those times when God bafflingly thwarts your plans, curtails your ministry, makes you ill or sad, or does any number of things that seem to fly in the face of gospel growth. This is what you should do. Take a photo of that baffling thing and stick it on a page next to a photo of some part of God's creation you find especially awesome or beautiful. Look at them side by side and remember that your trouble is an integral part of God's plan to perfect the universe. When you're gazing at a forest-cloaked mountainside in autumn, or the ocean sparkling in the morning, remind yourself that the God who made *that* made the previous two years of your life. One day it will all make glorious sense as you see how each broken heart and each broken plan plays its part in the great symphony of praise at the end of time.

The path of obedience is revealed to a people of no account

As verse 20 says, God has revealed his path to '*no* other nation'. The negative links back to the central proverb of verse 10. It reminds us that Israel was the least of all nations. And Israel's history of rebellion and failure only reinforces that point.

Here is some wisdom from this psalm for those times when praise feels far away, because troubles have made you unable to take notice of anything admirable. Write out verses 10 and 11 and remember that God delights in weakness, not strength, and in people who have no resources of their own to draw on. And with that in mind, tell him your troubles. Remember how he loves the prayer of the baby raven. If you can't pray, pray the Psalms, or use a psalm as a model to write a prayer. The words of lament you speak from the heart will delight him. He won't mind that David wrote them. The rabbis called even the laments 'praises'. And they were right. They are steps along the path of obedience.

The path of obedience ends in praise

The journey creates the destination. We can't always praise God for what we are enduring, but we know that the hardships of the path will make the arrival all the more exhilarating. You may find even in your cries of trouble that you are able to anticipate the end of the path with thankfulness (which is how laments typically end, of course).

Psalm 32 showed us that life is a series of gospel moments, of transitions from lament to praise that result from repentance and forgiveness. Each of those moments you go through in life is another reminder that thankfulness and praise is the end of the journey.

The LORD is a God who, with infinite power and wisdom, moves all creation to a single destined end: the lifting up of the humble, the sustaining of the weak, the rewarding of trust and hope. He has shown us the meaning of the universe in the resurrection of his Son, and now he sends that same word of power to the broken people who name Christ as Lord, so that in their long obedience through many trials and disappointments he may reveal his glory to the watching world. Praise the LORD!

Expanding circles of praise

The final three psalms, Psalms 148 – 150, give us three pictures of praise that progressively broaden our understanding of what praise means. We cannot read them now, but here is a brief guide for your own further reading and reflection.

Praise is being God's creature

Psalm 148 is a picture of every part of creation doing what it was made to do. Being who God made you to be is a species of praise, in the same way that your child praises you when she tells the truth as you raised her to do. Your obedience praises God by showing the world what he is like. And when every creature plays its proper part, creation as a whole will become one giant praising body.

Praise is announcing God's reign

Psalm 149 contains the striking image of the praises of God's people binding the world's rulers with shackles. The praises of the lowly bring down the proud. This is because praise declares who God is and how he acts in creation and redemption. It tears down false gods. It takes the powers that humans worship and claims them for God.[4] Specifically, praise confesses Christ as King. When we celebrate the resurrection we are challenging every other would-be ruler to bow before him. Gospel proclamation is a species of praise because the gospel tears down opposition to Christ and puts the world in order.

Praise is what your breath is for

Psalm 150 repeats the message we have heard a few times already: praise is the purpose of our existence. Its last line, 'Let everything that has breath praise the LORD,' refers back to the breath God breathed into humans at creation.

God gave us breath to breathe *in* and live, and to breathe *out* and speak. The basic sign of life in humans is breathing God's breath back to him in the form of words. Speech is the way others know us and we know others. Of course, a person can be alive without speaking (or even being able to speak), and a person can be alive without knowing God. But there's a close connection between the breath of God that makes us alive and the Spirit of God that makes us alive to him (see Ezekiel 37:9–14). We show that we are fully alive, alive in God, only when our breath sustains a relationship with him in words of praise.

For the moment, our praise is partial, fragmented and shrouded in ignorance. In the new creation, the risen Christ will be the face of God, the organizing centre, the single reference-point by which everything will fully understand itself and its relationship to everything else. We will know ourselves and others truly for the first time because we will see for the first time how all things are united under Christ. In a world like that, every wonderful detail we notice will be revealed as a wonderful truth about Jesus. All things will fill us with joy, and it will all be the joy of God, whose constancy and love and power and wisdom and perfection do not trample heedlessly over the world's pain but take it up and incorporate it into unimagined truth and beauty, with the Lamb that was slain at the centre. And as everything comes from him and leads back to him, and everything is summed up and completed in him, so we too are caught up into the joyous whole, not losing our selves, but freed to offer all that we are to the Christ who reigns in glory at the centre of it all. Praise the LORD!

I'll praise my Maker with my Breath;
And when my Voice is lost in Death,
  Praise shall employ my nobler Pow'rs:
My Days of Praise shall ne'er be past,
While Life, and Thought, and Being last,
  Or Immortality endures.[5]

Notes

1 Psalms 1 and 2: the journey begins

1 Unless otherwise stated, all biblical quotations are taken from the New International Version (Anglicized), 2011. All emphasis in biblical quotations is mine throughout.

2 Dietrich Bonhoeffer, *Psalms: The prayer book of the Bible*, tr. James H. Burtness (Minneapolis, MN: Augsburg, 1970), p. 25.

2 Psalm 32: weakness and gratitude

1 John Newton, *Olney Hymns, in Three Books* (London: W. Olivier, 1779), hymn xli.

2 John Bunyan, *The Pilgrim's Progress*, Oxford World Classics, ed. W. R. Owens (Oxford: Oxford University Press, 2003), p. 37.

3 Augustine, 'Exposition 2 of Psalm 31', in John E. Rotelle (ed.), *The Works of Saint Augustine: A translation for the 21st century*, Part III, vol. 15, tr. Marian Boulding (Hyde Park, NY: New City Press, 2000), p. 371.

4 The Order for Morning and Evening Prayer, *An Australian Prayer Book* (Sydney: Anglican Church of Australia, 1978), pp. 19–20.

5 Karl Barth, *The Faith of the Church* (London: SCM Press, 1958), pp. 157–158.

3 Psalm 69: suffering and hope

1 Augustine, *Expositions on the Book of Psalms*, Nicene and Post-Nicene Fathers, First Series, vol. 6, ed. Philip Schaff (Grand Rapids, MI: Eerdmans, 1956), p. 56.

2 Aramaic-speaking Jews had been providing oral translations of the Hebrew Bible in synagogues since long before Jesus' time. These

Aramaic 'Targums' were eventually written down by the rabbis. The Targum of Psalms was probably written down between the fourth and sixth centuries AD. See *The Targum of Psalms*, tr. David M. Stec, The Aramaic Bible, vol. 16 (Collegeville, MN: Liturgical Press, 2004), pp. 2, 134. Theodoret of Cyrus, *Commentary on the Psalms, 1–72*, tr. Robert C. Hill, The Fathers of the Church, vol. 101 (Washington, DC: Catholic University of America Press, 2000), p. 395.

3 I owe this insight to Bernd Janowski, *Arguing with God: A theological anthropology of the Psalms*, tr. Armin Siedlecki (Louisville, KY: Westminster John Knox Press, 2013), pp. 36–53.

4 *Unbreakable* (2000), directed by M. Night Shyamalan.

5 Andrew G. Shead and Andrew J. Cameron, 'Singing with the Messiah in a Foreign Land', in Andrew G. Shead (ed.), *Stirred by a Noble Theme: The book of Psalms in the life of the church* (Nottingham: Apollos, 2013), p. 170.

4 Psalm 88: despair and endurance

1 'Do not go gentle', *The Poems of Dylan Thomas* (New York, NY: New Directions, 1952).

2 Nicholas Wolterstorff, *Lament for a Son* (Grand Rapids, MI: Eerdmans, 1987), pp. 34–35.

3 Wolterstorff, *Lament for a Son*, p. 81.

4 The final two paragraphs have been adapted from Andrew Shead, 'A Church for Broken People', *Southern Cross: the news magazine for Sydney Anglicans* (September 2015), p. 11.

5 Psalm 91: the LORD is with you

1 <https://ourworldindata.org/excess-mortality-covid>.

2 Augustine, *Tractates on the Gospel of John 1–10*, tr. John W. Rettig, The Fathers of the Church, vol. 78 (Washington, DC: Catholic University of America Press, 1978), p. 211.

3 Jerome, *Letter 68.1*, Nicene and Post-Nicene Fathers, Second Series, vol. 6, ed. Philip Schaff (Peabody, MA: Hendrickson, 1995), p. 141, adapted.

6 Psalm 118: his love endures for ever

1 It comes from Erich Zenger, 'The Composition and Theology of the Fifth Book of Psalms, Psalms 107–145', *Journal for the Study of the Old Testament*, 80 (1998), pp. 77–102.

7 Psalm 147: what your breath is for

1 J. R. R. Tolkien, *The Return of the King* (London: George Allen & Unwin, 1955).

2 Edward Hirsch, *How to Read a Poem: And fall in love with poetry* (New York, NY: Harcourt, 1999), p. 75.

3 C-SPAN, 'Illinois State Senator Barack Obama 2004 Democratic National Convention Keynote Speech', video recording, 27 July 2004, online at <tinyurl.com/2p8342r8>.

4 These insights come from James L. Mays, *The Lord Reigns: A theological handbook to the Psalms* (Louisville, KY: Westminster John Knox Press, 1994), pp. 61–71.

5 I. Watts, *The Psalms of David Imitated in the Language of the New Testament* (London: J. Barker, 1784), p. 366.

Further resources and acknowledgments

There is more written on the Psalms than any other Old Testament book. What follows is a small selection of some resources I have found helpful for reading and interpreting the Psalms, plus some specific acknowledgments for quotes and influences in the preceding chapters.

Further resources

One good starting-point:

Christopher Ash, *Teaching Psalms, volume 1: From Text to Message* (London: Proclamation Trust Media, 2017)

Two concise commentaries:

Derek Kidner, *Psalms 1 – 72* and *Psalms 73 – 150* (London: IVP reprint, 2014)

James L. Mays, *Psalms* (Louisville, KY: Westminster John Knox Press, 2011)

Three historical and theological commentaries (on selected psalms):

Bruce K. Waltke, James M. Houston and Erika Moore, *The Psalms as Christian Worship* (Grand Rapids, MI: Eerdmans, 2010); *The Psalms as Christian Lament* (Grand Rapids, MI: Eerdmans, 2014); *The Psalms as Christian Praise* (Grand Rapids, MI: Eerdmans, 2019)

Four scholars who dig deep into the world of the Psalms:

Robert Alter, *The Art of Biblical Poetry*, rev. edn (New York, NY: Basic Books, 2011)

William P. Brown, *Seeing the Psalms: A theology of metaphor* (Louisville, KY: Westminster John Knox Press, 2002)

Bernd Janowski, *Arguing with God: A theological anthropology of the Psalms*, tr. Armin Siedlecki (Louisville, KY: Westminster John Knox Press, 2013)

Gordon J. Wenham, *Psalms as Torah: Reading biblical song ethically* (Grand Rapids, MI: Baker Academic, 2012) and *The Psalter Reclaimed: Praying and praising with the Psalms* (Wheaton, IL: Crossway, 2013)

Acknowledgments

I am especially grateful for the feedback Bruce Waltke has kindly given me on these studies; his probing questions have made this a better book. I also thank Tom Creedy, Mollie Barker and the team at IVP, who have put themselves out to guide this book expertly into print.

In addition to the works listed above, I have learned much from commentaries by Augustine, Luther, Calvin, Hans-Joachim Kraus, Frank Lothar Hossfeld, Erich Zenger, Peter Craigie, Marvin Tate, Leslie Allen, John Goldingay and others; and by the scholarly writings of many more, including Brian Brock, Susan Gillingham, Adam Hensley, Clinton McCann, Luis Alonso Schökel, Wilfred Watson and Gerald Wilson.

After completing this book, I belatedly read a helpful treatment of Luke's use of Psalms 2, 69, 91 and 118, which I recommend for those interested in digging deeper into the Christian meaning of these psalms: David B. Sloan, *Reading the Psalms with Jesus and the Apostles: The understanding of the Psalms in Luke–Acts* (Milton Keynes: Paternoster, 2018).